Jane Seymour

Jane Seymour

An Illustrated Life

Carol-Ann Johnston

PEN & SWORD
HISTORY

First published in Great Britain in 2023 by
Pen & Sword History
An imprint of Pen & Sword Books Limited
Yorkshire – Philadelphia

ISBN 978 1 39907 161 1

A CIP catalogue record for this book is
available from the British Library

Typeset by Mac Style
Printed in the UK by CPI Group (UK) Ltd, Croydon, CR0 4YY.

Pen & Sword Books Limited incorporates the imprints of After the
Battle, Atlas, Archaeology, Aviation, Discovery, Family History,
Fiction, History, Maritime, Military, Military Classics, Politics,
Select, Transport, True Crime, Air World, Frontline Publishing,
Leo Cooper, Remember When, Seaforth Publishing, The Praetorian
Press, Wharncliffe Local History, Wharncliffe Transport,
Wharncliffe True Crime and White Owl.

For a complete list of Pen & Sword titles please contact

PEN & SWORD BOOKS LIMITED
47 Church Street, Barnsley, South Yorkshire, S70 2AS, England
E-mail: enquiries@pen-and-sword.co.uk
Website: www.pen-and-sword.co.uk
or
PEN AND SWORD BOOKS
1950 Lawrence Rd, Havertown, PA 19083, USA
E-mail: Uspen-and-sword@casematepublishers.com
Website: www.penandswordbooks.com

Contents

Preface

Ifirst learned about the Six Wives of Henry VIII when I was at primary school. I remember thinking six queens was pretty amazing and, as I got older, I became even more fascinated, or obsessed, with them, but one has always stood out to me: Jane Seymour.

Jane is often overlooked in favour of her predecessors and, at first glance, it's not hard to see why: next to Catherine Howard she is the least documented wife of Henry VIII. She was quiet and reserved, kept her thoughts and opinions to herself, only offering them on rare occasions, and she did not cause a stir. This has led to her being dismissed as an uninteresting person in her own right, a fact that seems most unfair. Whilst the documentation we have for Jane is slight, there is enough to construct a picture of her – and who is to say more will not be found? Artwork, artifacts and texts once thought lost can reappear in the most extraordinary circumstances.

I started my page, 'Jane Seymour Henry VIII's Third Wife', in order to bring more attention to Jane and to show that she is just as worthy of attention as any of the other wives. Interestingly, this was on 1 March 2012, making the page ten years old at the time of writing.

When I was younger, I was quite shy, I did not really interact with people outside of my friendship group unless I was approached nor did I like to be the centre of attention, and it strikes me Jane was perhaps very similar. By coincidence, we also share some physical characteristics: I am also fair haired and pale skinned with light blue eyes.

Jane Seymour witnessed one of the most turbulent chapters in English history. Queen for just under seventeen months, her reign was spent treading carefully and acting as a peacemaker or reconciler; she had little power but proved an excellent wife for the temperamental Henry. At the time of their marriage Henry was well on his way to becoming the tyrant we know, whereas Jane has often been described as kind, virtuous, gentle and amiable and it is likely she received the affection Henry could no longer inspire from his people. As the eventual mother of the heir to the throne, she secured his love and respect by giving him his heart's desire.

This is her story.

Close-up of the Mortimer lion displaying Queen Jane Seymour's badge (part of the king's beasts at the entrance of Hampton Court Palace). (*Author's Collection*)

Chapter 1

The Seymour Family

The early history of the Seymour family, or St Maur as the name was originally written, is vague, to say the least. It is believed they themselves traced their lineage back to the village of Touraine, Saint-Maur-sur-Loire, to a gentleman called Richard de St Maur who was the head of the village in the seventh or eighth century. We then find a Guy de St Maur who may have been Richard's son, who appears in the Battle Abbey Roll, paying homage for his lands to the Abbey of Villers. After this the trail goes cold but there is a mention of a Ludo de St Maur in 919, who leads us to Goscelin de St Maur whom we have written evidence for as his name is listed in the Charter of Foulque Marte in the year 1000; he also received a letter from the Pope of the time, Pope Gregory VII. Goscelin married and had four sons; however, it is the second son, Guillaume, who provides us with the link to Jane Seymour. Guillaume had a son called Wido de St Maur who appears to have arrived in England with William the Conqueror in 1066.

We cannot be entirely sure of this as the documents are incomplete but David Loades found that Wido received a barony which extended into Somerset, Wiltshire and Gloucestershire. Jump forward a few hundred years and we find a Jane Seymour at the court of Henry VIII who was from Wiltshire. Wido appears to have died before 1087 where the records show that his barony was now held by his son, William Fitz Wido. Sadly, the records are vague again but it seems William had a son Roger who may have had a connection to the Welsh Marches but this is speculation. We then find a Bartolomew de Sancto Mauro (possibly Roger's son) witnessing a charter in around 1170 and then his son listed as one of King Henry II's esquires. Fast forward to the reign of the last son of Henry II, King John, and we find a record of a Milo de St Maur forcing the king to sign the Magna Carta.[1]

Milo produced two sons, Geoffrey and William, and it is William's line that produced Jane Seymour. It appears there was some sort of break

The Seymour panther displaying the arms of Seymour: gules, two wings conjoined in lure or (part of the king's beasts at the entrance of Hampton Court Palace). (*Author's Collection*)

between the two St Maur lines as both sides appear to have denied any connection with each other for an unknown reason. David Loades suggests that Milo perhaps married twice;[2] if this is what happened, then it appears, as with some second marriages today, the two half-brothers did not get along and later went their separate ways.

With the arrival of William on the scene, we are on much firmer ground with the St Maur/ Seymour connection to the Welsh Marches. In 1235, William entered into a dubious agreement with Gilbert Marshall, Earl of Pembroke, to take the manor of Undy from the Welshman Morgan ap Howell; the plan appears to have been for the two men to split the manor equally between them. William paid the earl a fee for his share but retained the right of possession whenever circumstances arose. Whilst all this is very morally dubious, by English Law of the time it was perfectly legal.

William's first priority appears to have remained Penhow Castle as he enlarged and rebuilt the property and established a large park for hunting. He also built a church dedicated to Abbott St Maur, the family's patron saint,[3] though later the saint would change to St John the Baptist.

Apart from the agreement regarding the manor of Undy, there appears to have been a 'regular' relationship with the Earl of Pembroke's kin; William's name appears on several charters in connection to Gilbert and Walter Marshall, kin of the earl, and he married a daughter of the Earl of Pembroke. Nothing more is known of William and he appears to have passed away by 1269 when the Lord of the Manor of Undy is now a Sir Roger de St Maur.[4]

As has become familiar, the records for Roger show very little, only that he produced a son, another Roger, who then went on to marry a daughter of Damarel of Devonshire, Joan. The couple produced two sons, John and another Roger. John would produce his own son, another Roger, who would go on to have a daughter whose name is not known who married into the Bowlays of Monmouthshire – through her Penhow Castle was conveyed to the Bowlays.

John's brother Roger retained the Manor of Undy and he married Cecilia, a daughter of John de Beauchamp, Baron of Hache, who coincidentally was descended from William Marshall, Earl of Pembroke, strengthening again the links between the two families. Cecilia and her sister were the co-heiresses to their father's estate and when he died in

1363, his lands were divided up between them; however, Roger died prior to this. Cecilia appears to have outlived her eldest son William as well.[5]

We have a record of this William being in attendance to the Prince of Wales, Edward, the Black Prince, in Gascony and he married the daughter of Simon de Brockburn, Margaret. The couple produced a son who went onto marry Maud, the daughter and co-heir to the knight Sir William Estuary. It was through Maud that the Seymour residence of Wolf Hall (or Wulfhall as it was then known) entered the family; Maud's family had been the hereditary Wardens of Savernake Forest since the reign of Henry III of England and were the bearers of the symbolic hunting horn that signified their status. Roger inherited this too. When Roger died, his son John Seymour inherited his vast collection of properties and responsibilities.[6]

This John Seymour became Sheriff of Hampshire and later Wiltshire as well during the minority of the ill-fated Henry VI; he was knighted in 1432. In 1434, he was elected Sheriff of Gloucester and Somerset, which shows how prominent the Seymour family now was, as sheriffs were mainly elected from the largest landowners in the area. In 1440, he sat in Parliament for Wiltshire and in 1454 was a member of the commission of array aimed at raising a force against the Duke of York. John served on many commissions between 1453 and 1459 and barring one small blip in 1458 when he was granted a pardon for allowing a felon to escape, appears to have been a solid, reliable servant of the crown.[7] John married Isabel, a daughter of Mark Williams of Bristol, in 1424, producing a son, another John who predeceased him. The younger John Seymour had lived long enough to marry Elizabeth, daughter of Sir Robert Coker of Laurence Lydiard, with whom he had two sons, John and Humphrey.

It is this John Seymour we are interested in: he inherited Wolf Hall but did not serve on any commissions until after 1480, and also rather prudently he did not take sides in the troubles of 1483 when the House of York was tearing itself apart. During the short reign of Richard III, he was recorded as a commissioner of array for Wiltshire, at a time when there were many threats to Richard's throne. By 1485, John had been granted a survey of the bounds of Savernake Forest; he also served on a commission to deal with rioters in Wiltshire.[8]

In 1486, the first Tudor king, Henry VII, cleared up an anomaly in his position which seems not to have been corrected when John reached his majority. The new king granted John the livery and right to his grandfather's estates. It is interesting to note that Henry VII did this as he was barely two years into his reign and was never quick to offer or confirm grants, even ones that were inherited; he was more concerned about an alternative power base being built in opposition to him so John must have impressed him or proved his loyalty.

John married twice, first to Elizabeth Darrell, the daughter of Sir George Darrell, with whom he had four sons and four daughters. His second marriage to Margaret, a daughter of Robert Hardon, only produced one son, Roger Seymour. The four sons from his first marriage all enjoyed careers under the Tudors: the second son George was Sheriff of Wiltshire in 1499; the third son William was made a Knight of the Bath on the marriage of Prince Arthur to the Princess of Spain, Catherine of Aragon; and the fourth son Roger (not to be confused with his half-brother from his father's second marriage) rose to be a Gentleman Usher of the Chamber. The eldest son of his first marriage was named after his father, John Seymour. This John Seymour would be the father of Jane Seymour, third queen of Henry VIII.[9]

Chapter 2

Lady Jane Seymour

At the time of the elder John's death in 1491, Jane's father had not reached his majority. Curiously, an inquisition was held in 1492 to establish what lands the elder John held in Somerset and who his heir was, a process that was not repeated in Wiltshire where Jane's father appeared to inherit without problem. The younger John's wardship and marriage was granted to Sir Henry Wentworth in 1493. John would marry a daughter of Sir Henry, Lady Margery, sometime before 1498: Lady Margery would be Jane's mother.[1]

Sir John Seymour by an unknown artist, year unknown. Jane's father was never prominent at court and it's not known how close the two were.

Oil painting based on a brass rubbing of Elizabeth Cheney by Wentworth Huyshe, the woman who connected Jane Seymour, Anne Boleyn and Catherine Howard.

An illuminated manuscript miniature of Edward III from the 1430 Bruges Garter Book made by William Bruges (1375–1450), first Garter King of Arms, British Library, c. 1430–50. Jane was descended from Edward III through her mother.

Lady Margery Wentworth was the second daughter of Sir Henry Wentworth and Anne Say. Anne was the second daughter of Elizabeth Cheney from her second marriage, to Sir John Say. Cheney had first married Sir Frederick Tilney in 1445 but their marriage ended with his death in 1446 and the couple only produced a daughter, Elizabeth, Anne's half-sister. Elizabeth Tilney would go onto marry Thomas Howard, Earl of Surrey, later second Duke of Norfolk, and with him have nine children including Thomas, Elizabeth and Edmund Howard. Thomas Howard would become the third Duke of Norfolk, whilst Elizabeth and Edmund would, like Margery, go onto be the mother and father of two of Henry's queens: Elizabeth was the mother of Anne Boleyn, Edmund the father of Catherine Howard. Jane Seymour, Anne Boleyn and Catherine Howard were therefore half-second cousins.

Margery brought the all-important drop of royal blood to her new family as she was descended from Edward III through his son Lionel of Antwerp, 1st Duke of Clarence. Margery served in the household of her aunt, Elizabeth Tilney, the Countess of Surrey. Whilst in her aunt's household, she became the muse of the poet John Skelton who immortalised her in his poem, the *Garland of Laurel*. Skelton praised her demeanour, describing her as a shy and kind girl, also comparing her to the primrose and the columbine. Margery was widely regarded as a great beauty by Skelton and others; sadly for Jane it would appear she inherited her mother's personality but not her looks.[2]

Sir John was knighted in 1497 after serving Henry VII at the Battle of Blackheath, and that same year he became the Sheriff of Wiltshire, holding the office until 1498. From 1499 he was named as a Commissioner of the Peace for Wiltshire, a position he held until his death. Sir John was never a large presence at the Royal Court unlike some of his children; most of his career was confined to Wiltshire and the surrounding areas. He was the steward to the Duke of Buckingham in 1503, then became the Sheriff of Wiltshire twice more, from 1507–8 and 1525–6, and the Sheriff of Somerset and Dorset between 1515–16 and 1526–7. He is recorded as being a subsidy commissioner for Wiltshire in 1512, 1514 and 1525, as well as for both the town and county of Salisbury in 1524. He would be named on just about every commission for the rest of his life.

In 1509, Henry VII died and the throne passed to his second son Prince Henry, now Henry VIII. His elder brother Prince Arthur had died suddenly and unexpectedly in 1502 not long after his marriage to Catherine of Aragon. At this time Sir John was a knight of the body to the new king but this is believed to have been in recognition of his importance in Wiltshire rather than any close intimacy to the new king

Westminster Abbey. Plans were put in place for Jane's coronation in the abbey but after two postponements following an outbreak of the plague and the uprising now known as the Pilgrimage of Grace, she was never crowned. She would likely have been crowned soon after Edward's VI birth had she survived. (*Author's Collection*)

personally. Over twenty years later he was created a Groom of the Privy chamber but again this was more in recognition of his prominence in Wiltshire. He attended the funeral of Henry VII, receiving a livery grant, and curiously both he and his wife are listed in a pardon roll of Henry VIII. There is no surviving evidence of misconduct – this may have been a general pardon to cover anyone who had held the position of sheriff in the previous reign.

On 11 June 1509 Henry VIII married his brother's widow and the pair were crowned together in Westminster Abbey on 24 June. Catherine had made a good impression on the people of England during her short tenure as Princess of Wales, and as the new Queen of England she was welcomed with open arms. In 1511 Catherine gave birth to a prince named Henry after his father; tragically, she had already suffered a still birth in 1510 and confusion and lack of understanding surrounding pregnancy at the time led physicians, and Catherine, to think she was still pregnant with a twin but no child ever came. Tragedy struck again when Prince Henry died after only living for fifty-two days. At the prince's funeral Sir John carried a banner, a sign of favour.[3]

In 1512, Sir John took on a more military-based role, serving with Sir Charles Brandon on a ship called the *Dragon of Greenwich* though it is unclear if he ever sailed on her. In 1513, he is listed as leading 100 men in the Brittany campaign but it is believed his role here was changed and redirected to the royal army in Picardy – he was definitely a witness to the Battle of the Spurs and the siege of Therouanne; he was awarded a knight bannernet shortly after for his bravery. He again served with Charles Brandon, now Duke of Suffolk, in France in 1523.

Sir John witnessed the glorious event known now as the Field of the Cloth of Gold in 1520, a meeting between Henry VIII and the French king, Francis I, though there is no record that Margery was in attendance on the queen. He was also present at a meeting with the Emperor Charles V (Catherine of Aragon's nephew); there were actually two meetings – before and after the meeting with Francis I. He was well regarded enough to accompany the emperor personally at the second meeting.[4]

Monumental brass of John Seymour, (died 15 July 1510), eldest son of Sir John Seymour and Margery Wentworth. Jane was probably not old enough to remember him.

Sir John is listed as serving on the commission appointed to assess the possessions of the disgraced Cardinal Thomas Wolsey in 1529. He returned to France in 1532 escorting the king and his future wife, the Marquess of Pembroke, Anne Boleyn. This appears to be the last 'big' event he took part in.

In the meantime, Sir John and Lady Margery had been producing a family of their own. It is believed the couple had ten children, six sons and four daughters, though as with most families in Tudor times, not all would reach adulthood. Their firstborn was a son named after his father, but there is little evidence to suggest he lived beyond childhood. It is the couple's second son Edward who is widely remembered as the eldest Seymour child. Edward was followed by two more brothers, Henry and Thomas. The couple's fifth child was their first daughter, Jane, and she was followed by another two daughters, Elizabeth and Dorothy. The other three children were another John, Anthony and Margery, though there is little surviving evidence of them so it is assumed they died young, perhaps even younger than their elder brother John.[5]

Edward, as the eldest surviving son, was the heir and hope of the family's future. Born in about 1500, he attended Henry VIII's sister, Mary, as a page of honour when she travelled to France to marry Francis I's predecessor, Louis XII. When he returned from France, he is believed to have attended the universities of Oxford and Cambridge but if he did there is no surviving record and no evidence of him taking a degree. After being knighted in 1523, Edward became an esquire of the King's Household in 1524. In 1525, he moved to join the household of the king's illegitimate son, Henry Fitzroy, Duke of Richmond and

Edward Seymour, later 1st Duke of Somerset, by a follower of François Clouet, c. sixteenth century. After Henry's death Edward became the Lord Protector on his young nephew's behalf but would later be removed from office and eventually executed.

Somerset, as Master of the Horse, a position of great responsibility as the Master of the Horse was responsible for the household's travel arrangements, which in Tudor times inevitably involved a lot of horses. It also ensured a degree of closeness to the boy he was serving; if things had gone differently, Edward may have stayed with him throughout his career; however, everything in England changed as a result of Henry VIII's quest for a legitimate son.[6] Little is known about Henry; unlike Edward and Thomas, he appears to have preferred a country life to a court one. Possibly born in 1503, a Harry Seymour was living in St John's Parish, Winchester, in 1524, when he was assessed on 10 marks in wages for the subsidy. If it's the same Henry Seymour, he appears to have served the Bishop of Winchester, Richard Fox, as his name survives on a list that includes others known to have served the archbishop. By 1526, he had become the Keeper of Taunton Castle and had entered royal service, possibly thanks to Edward's influence. He married Barbara Wolfe, the daughter of Morgan Wolfe, and the couple had three sons and seven daughters.[7]

Thomas Seymour was Jane's final surviving brother born in around 1508, and like Henry we know very little about his early life but he was probably educated at home by the family chaplain. Thomas arrived at Henry's court sometime before 1530 in the service of a kinsman, Sir Francis Bryan. Sir Francis was a courtier and diplomat at Henry's court but also served Henry as an ambassador. In 1532, Thomas was rewarded for delivering letters to him whilst he was an envoy in France. That same year he received a significant grant, Forester of Enfield Chase. Thomas may not have been as well known as Edward but he was certainly capable enough to manage on his own and, whilst, like his elder brother, he received preferment after his sister became queen – he did not solely rely on her.[8]

Thomas Seymour by Nicolas Denizot, c. 1547–9. Thomas would never achieve the prominence of his elder brother Edward but it was not for lack of trying; he was executed during his nephew's reign after being accused of thirty-three counts of treason.

Elizabeth was born around 1518 and Dorothy in around 1519. Like her brother Henry, little is known of Dorothy's life except that she was married twice, first to Sir Clement Smith with whom she had seven children and second to Thomas Leventhorpe with whom she had another six children, proving to contemporaries that their belief that the Seymours were notoriously fertile was justified.[9]

These were Jane's brothers and sisters, the people she grew up with. They didn't know it then but each of them had a personal relationship and connection to the future Queen of England. We don't know when Jane was born but it is estimated to have been between 1507 and 1509. The years 1507 and 1508 are supported by the number of ladies that reportedly walked in procession at her funeral in 1537 – Jane had twenty-nine. Jane's later ally, the Imperial Ambassador, Eustace Chapuys, described her as over 25 in 1536,[10] but doesn't reveal any more than that. Birth registration was not compulsory in England until 1538 but it is doubtful even if it had been that records would have survived this long to show the exact date of Jane's and her siblings' births.

Little is known of Jane's upbringing. She was most likely born and raised at Wolf Hall, the Seymour family seat. Nothing of the home Jane knew survives above ground; however, recent excavations have revealed the original foundations still remain (the Wolf Hall building that stands on the land today was built in the seventeenth century). A survey from Edward VI's reign reveals that the property comprised 1,263 acres of land and was a working farm. The land would have been used for pasture and crops but the property would also have had gardens and orchards.[11] The last surviving bit of the property Jane would have recognised was an old barn that burned down in the 1920s; legend tells us that Henry and Jane held a feast there to celebrate their marriage, and tourists were shown old nails in the walls that supposedly held the decorations from that celebration.[12]

In a time when children of noble houses were sent to other households at about the age of 7 in order for them to develop new skills (as a type of training or apprenticeship), there is no evidence of this for Jane and her sisters.[13] It was once believed that Jane served in the household of Henry VIII's sister Mary after she became Queen of France but there is no evidence to support that she ever left England. We have to assume that Jane and her sisters remained at home with their mother and learned what they needed to under her direction: sewing, household management, accounts, music, outdoor pursuits and proper behaviour for a young lady.[14] Women were expected to be chaste and devout so that no slur could attach itself to their reputations and jeopardise their futures. Margery would have warned her daughters to always be 'sad, sober, wise and discreet'.

Jane was regarded as an expert needlewoman and some of her work survived in the Royal Household until 1652 when it was returned to a descendant of her brother Edward. The items

Portrait miniature of Jane Seymour by Nicholas Hilliard after Hans Holbein the Younger, date unknown.

consisted of 'Five pieces of Chequard hangings of coarse making, having the Duke of Somerset's Arms in them, And one furniture of a bed of Needlework with a chaise and cushions suitable thereunto'.[15] As queen she enjoyed following the hunt and it is likely her skills at hunting and riding came from her upbringing.

Alongside her mother's teaching, Jane most likely received a rudimentary education at the hands of the family chaplain; whilst in the past she has been dismissed as illiterate, there is evidence she could read and write in English (her signature survives) and she appears to have understood some French and possibly a little Latin but she was never fluent in the latter two – in fairness to her she had no need to be. Jane was not raised with the expectation of being on the European stage or even a star of the royal court; she was raised to make a good match to improve her family's connections, a loyal wife and helpmeet to her husband and to manage her husband's and household's interests; she would also supervise the bringing up of her children.

What has puzzled historians for many years is that Jane's younger sister Elizabeth was married first. Daughters were traditionally married off in age order, so Jane as the elder should have been married first. There have been many theories as to why this didn't happen with Jane and Elizabeth: dowry, education, compatibility or, heartbreakingly, appearance. I think we can dismiss dowry because if Sir John could provide one for one daughter, why not the other? With three daughters to provide dowries for, money would have been stretched but the indisputable fact is that he was able to provide for Elizabeth. All three daughters would have received the same education from their mother so this cannot have been a factor. When we think about compatibility and appearance, we get onto slightly firmer ground. Almost all marriages were arranged in Tudor times but if the couple were really incompatible and did not like each other, it was not forced on them. From what we know of Jane's character, she was regarded as a quiet and dutiful woman and as Henry VIII himself

Portrait of a lady probably of the Cromwell family, possibly Elizabeth Seymour by Hans Holbein the Younger, c. 1535–40. The sitter does bear a resemblance to the most famous portrait of Jane as queen.

later noted, a peacemaker; it seems unlikely that she would have caused a fuss over a match her parents had made unless her suitor did.

Sadly, it may have come down to appearance. Jane was not regarded as a beauty and has often been referred to as the original 'Plain Jane'. An unidentified portrait in the Toledo Museum of Art shows a woman dressed in sumptuous black cloth with beautiful jewellery. The portrait has previously been identified as the tragic Catherine Howard, Henry VIII's fifth queen, but that identity has been disputed; in fact, the portrait is identified in the collection as 'A Lady, probably a member of the Cromwell family'. The consensus today is that it could be a portrait of Elizabeth after her marriage to Thomas Cromwell's son.[16] The sitter certainly bears a facial resemblance to the most famous portrait of Jane Seymour painted by Hans Holbein but her features are softer and she has more colour to her face. Perhaps it was something as small as this that resulted in Elizabeth marrying first.

Even one of Jane's biggest supporters, Eustace Chapuys, was unsure what Henry saw in his future wife and he (Chapuys) had every reason to complement Jane as a fellow supporter of the Princess Mary. Whilst Jane has been described as having fair hair and blue eyes, the features that were the epitome of beauty at the time, it is possible she may have been too pale and too fair haired – but then beauty is often in the eye of the beholder. Henry clearly saw something in Jane he liked enough to fall for her and later marry her. Whether it was a combination of behaviour, personality, looks or that unknown something, we will probably never know.

Chapter 3

At Court

Jane arrived at court sometime between 1527 and 1529; how she secured her place is unknown, although there are three equally plausible theories. Whilst the Seymours were not one of the notable families at Henry's court, they had served him for a number of years in various ways. Lady Margery served Queen Catherine during her early years as Henry's consort and whilst there is no surviving record of a close relationship, it would have been enough of a connection to act as a recommendation. Sir John had been present at the sieges of Therouanne and Tournay in 1513 and the couple's eldest son Edward was considered a rising star, making connections and friends at court. Jane may even, at a later-than-usual age, have served in the household of a noble lady before transferring to Catherine's household.

It's also possible she received a recommendation from Sir Francis Bryan, who later ensured her a place in Queen Anne's household, so it's not unlikely he was able to do so a few years earlier. Sir Francis, like Charles Brandon, Duke of Suffolk, was a rare lifelong friend of Henry VIII and always retained his favour.[1] Interestingly, he was a cousin of Anne Boleyn, Jane Seymour and Catherine Howard, but he seems to have been closer to Jane and the Seymours. The Seymours were not as well connected as the Howards and Boleyns, so Sir Francis may have decided to 'lend a hand' but it is interesting to think that perhaps there was a friendlier relationship with the Seymours and Jane. After all, if he did help Jane get a place at

Jane Seymour portrait miniature by Lucas Horenbout, c. 1536/7.

Portrait of Jane Seymour by Cornelius Vermeulen after Adriaen Van Der Werff, c. 1697.

court, it was at a time when she was unknown and would not benefit him in any way. Sir Francis would also later turn against Anne and side with Jane in the events of 1536.

Once Jane arrived at court, she would have been sworn in to the Queen's Household and then provided with lodgings and shown her duties. This must have been equally a nerve-wracking and exciting time for Jane; if she had never left home before, the court must have seemed daunting with so many different people of various ranks that required skill and tact to navigate. As there are no surviving reports or stories of Jane offending someone in her youth after she became queen, which would have been the time they would have spread, we have to assume that she was able to learn quickly and adapt to this new world. It seems she did it so well that she went almost unnoticed until later.

As Jane was going to be serving the Queen of England, she would have required a whole new wardrobe, as what she had at worn at home at Wolf Hall would not have been grand enough.[2] Did she feel a young woman's excitement at having beautiful new clothes, or did she take it all in her stride and accept it almost as a uniform? As queen she was required to be even more grandly dressed but as you will see, there are hints of a woman who loved fine clothes and jewellery for their own sake.

Who was Catherine of Aragon, the queen Jane was about to serve? Catherine was the youngest child of the 'Catholic Kings' Isabella of Castile and Ferdinand of Aragon and she and her siblings were widely regarded as the finest matches in Europe. Henry VIII's father had been able to secure an agreement with Catherine's parents that she would marry his son and heir but it was not Henry

Formerly identified as Catherine Parr, in 2012 this portrait was re-identified as Catherine of Aragon, Henry VIII's first wife, by an unknown artist, c. sixteenth century. Whilst serving Catherine, Jane came to love and admire her and would remain loyal to her daughter Mary after Catherine's death.

the monarchs were thinking of but his elder brother Prince Arthur. After years of negotiations Catherine arrived in England in 1501 and the two were married, and soon after the young Prince and Princess of Wales travelled to Arthur's base in the Welsh Marches, Ludlow Castle, to establish their household. Tragically, the marriage only lasted five months as both Arthur and Catherine fell ill with an unknown illness. Catherine recovered but Arthur did not. In order to salvage the alliance, Henry, Isabella and Ferdinand all agreed that Catherine should marry Arthur's younger brother, Prince Henry, now the heir to the throne.

After a frustrating and difficult widowhood where money was tight and Catherine's status fluctuated due to varying political and familial circumstances, Henry VII died in 1509 and his son ascended the throne as King Henry VIII. He decided almost instantly that he was going to uphold his promise and past agreement to marry Catherine. In the early years it was a genuinely happy marriage and both seemed to have been in love with each other; they had many shared interests and had both been educated to a high standard, allowing them to converse equally on a wide range of subjects. Catherine proved herself fertile by falling pregnant numerous times but seemed to struggle to produce a healthy child. After the loss of their son Prince Henry, both parents were grief stricken but it was noted that Henry was especially solicitous of Catherine – he did not blame her, anyone else or any circumstance at this time. Tragedy was to follow tragedy as Catherine's next two pregnancies ended with a boy who was stillborn and another boy who was either stillborn or lived only a few hours after birth. Finally, in 1516, Catherine gave birth to a daughter the couple called Mary, who lived beyond her first years and looked sure to survive. The couple were relieved and Henry was recorded as saying, 'We are both young; if it was a daughter this time, by the grace of God the sons will follow.'[3] Sadly, they never did. Catherine became pregnant once more in 1518 but gave birth prematurely to a daughter who did not live; it was the last pregnancy she would have.

It is sometimes forgotten that Catherine was older than Henry by five years, and after repeated childbirths that damaged her health and figure, she looked a lot older than her still-youthful-looking husband. Whilst there wasn't a break in the marriage, the couple drifted apart and Catherine became more devout; she fasted, wore a hair shirt under her robes, went to confession three times a week and prayed kneeling on the cold stone floor without a cushion. She would also rise at midnight to be present at Matins. Her other focus was her daughter and she ensured that Mary received an education that was fit for a future queen in her own right, not just a consort. Catherine was described as 'affable in conversation, courteous to all, and of an excellent and pious disposition'.[4] This was the woman Jane served and grew to admire; and on whom she would later model her own court as queen.

Jane's arrival coincided with the beginning of 'the King's Great Matter'; she was about to witness some of the most shocking and astounding events in England's history. She had no idea she would later be a part of them.

Chapter 4

The King's Great Matter

Catherine had not produced a son and after 1518 it appeared unlikely that she would ever have another pregnancy. Henry VIII was faced with the probability that when he died, his throne would be inherited by his only surviving legitimate child, the Princess Mary. England, unlike France, did not prohibit women from inheriting the throne but to say the prospect of a queen regnant was less than ideal (or wanted) would be an understatement. The last woman to try to claim the throne of England in her own right was the Empress Matilda, daughter of Henry I. Her brother had been killed in the *White Ship* disaster of 1120 and, apart from Matilda, Henry I had no other legitimate children. Henry made his court swear an oath of loyalty to his daughter and her successors but the move was never popular and when Henry died, Matilda's cousin Stephen seized the throne with the backing of the magnates and the English Church. This act started a war between the two claimants which would only end with the death of King Stephen's son Eustace in unrelated circumstances and his decision to recognise Matilda's son as his heir. Matilda's son was the future Henry II, that dynamic, energetic and sometimes ruthless ruler who expanded England's territories and influence and created the Plantagenet dynasty.[1]

Kings were expected to be able to lead their country, they were required to command armies, devise plans, negotiate treaties and most importantly of all retain power and the throne itself. England had a very recent history of turbulence as the throne had switched repeatedly between Lancastrian and Yorkist rule – the warring royal houses had almost torn England apart and the people were war-weary. All they wanted was strong and able governance and whatever the faults of Henry VIII and his father, they can at least claim they provided that.

If Henry had looked back to Matilda and her son for inspiration, he could have married Mary off as soon as she reached a suitable age; she could have produced children, ideally a son and so the throne would have been inherited by Henry VIII's grandson, not his son. The problem with this was whom was Mary to marry; whomever she married, it would be her husband in control and his family that she would become a part of, therefore the throne would be inherited by a new dynasty, not an outcome Henry wanted.

Or he could promote his illegitimate son? During his marriage to Catherine, Henry VIII did have mistresses though he was more discreet than his French counterpart Francis I, so discreet that we can't be sure now who they definitely were. However, in 1519, Lady Elizabeth Blount, or Bessie as she was known, gave birth to a son who was immediately recognised by the king; the baby was named Henry Fitzroy (Fitzroy meaning 'son of a king') and later he would become known as the Duke of Richmond,[2] the title Henry VII was known by before he became king.

Fitzroy was the only illegitimate child Henry ever acknowledged, leaving us wondering if, like his mistresses, he ever had more illegitimate children but never recognised them.

Rumours spread that Henry was considering making Fitzroy his heir but we'll never know how seriously he contemplated this as at about this time Henry fell in love … and it wasn't with his wife. No one, not even Henry, would foresee the effects this love affair would have on his family and England.

Anne Boleyn was the younger daughter of Sir Thomas Boleyn and Lady Elizabeth Howard, and through her mother she was related to one of the most prestigious houses in England, the Howards, making her a niece of the Duke of Norfolk. Despite

Near-contemporary painting at Hever Castle of Anne Boleyn, Henry VIII's second wife, artist unknown, c. 1550. Anne's marriage to Henry changed England forever but she was never popular with her subjects who still regarded Catherine of Aragon as England's Queen. Anne was a cousin of Catherine Howard and half-second cousin to Jane but they were never close as Jane remained a supporter Catherine of Aragon.

later rumours to the contrary, Thomas Boleyn was a respected and able diplomat in his own right and did not rely on his daughter to advance his career. He travelled abroad various times on behalf of both Henry VII and Henry VIII and made a particularly good impression on Margaret of Austria, the Regent of the Netherlands.

Margaret was the daughter of the Holy Roman Emperor, Maximilian, and Mary, Duchess of Burgundy, and was widely regarded as one of the most capable women of her time. She had received a fine education in France in preparation for her future as its queen consort but her betrothed Charles VIII broke off the agreement. Instead, Margaret married the Prince of Asturias and Girona, Juan, the only son of Isabella of Castile and Ferdinand of Aragon; she was therefore a sister-in-law of Queen Catherine. Tragically, this marriage ended suddenly with the death of Juan in October 1497 and the loss of their child during a premature labour. In 1501, Margaret married again, to Philibert II, Duke of Savoy, but this marriage was destined to end early as well, with the duke dying of pleurisy in 1504. During her time as Duchess of Savoy, Margaret gained valuable experience governing which would serve her well in her future role as regent for her nephew Charles V, the future Holy Roman Emperor. Due to the size of his inheritance, Charles would need to rely on relatives to help him govern. Margaret was educated, able, cultured and excelled in diplomacy and she would govern for Charles in various ways for the rest of her life.

Perhaps Margaret recognised a kindred spirit in Anne; whatever it was, Margaret offered to take Anne into her household and further her education. Margaret's court was considered one of the most cultured and refined courts during the renaissance and she often took on young girls and gave them an exemplary education. Anne excelled there. She was taught arithmetic, reading, spelling, writing, grammar and history. Margaret did not forget the domestic skills either and ensured that Anne was taught household management, needlework, good manners, music and singing. It was not all studying and hard work though as her charges also learned horseback riding, falconry, hunting and archery, and for gentler pastimes the ladies were taught to play chess and cards. Anne made a favourable impression on Margaret who wrote to her father, stating she was 'so presentable and so pleasant, considering her youthful age, that I am more beholden to you for sending her to me, than you to me'.[3] Anne remained at Margaret's court until 1513 when her father arranged for her to travel to France to serve its future queen, Mary, the younger sister of Henry VIII. England and France had signed a peace treaty and one of the stipulations was the marriage of Louis XII and Mary to ensure the alliance and friendship of the two countries. Louis, like Henry VIII, had no son and he hoped to produce one with his young bride. Anne did not serve Mary long as Louis died three months after the marriage, some said due to overexertion in the bedroom but more likely due to gout. The couple did not produce a child.

After Louis's death Anne transferred to the new Queen's Household, Queen Claude, a daughter of Louis whose husband was now the King of France as Francis I. Anne would serve Claude for the next seven years, finishing off her education and becoming fluent in French. During her time in France, she absorbed its culture, art and fashion; later it was commented that she could be taken for a born Frenchwoman and she started many new trends in the court of England.[4] She developed a lifelong interest in literature, music and religious philosophy and became skilled in the art of courtly love.

Anne's most prominent biographer, Eric Ives, suggests that during her time in France Anne may have been acquainted with Francis I's sister, Marguerite of Navarre, an author in her own right and a patron of reformers and humanists. It is interesting to speculate that Anne's knowledge and belief in reform may have been influenced by Marguerite and that it was from her that Anne may have picked up ideas for her future battle with the Papacy.

Anne's time in France came to an end in 1522 when she was recalled to England by her father who was negotiating a marriage for her with a cousin, an Irishman named James Butler. The marriage was intended to settle the dispute over the Earldom of Ormond after the death of the 7th Earl; Anne's father believed he had the right to it as the son of former earl's eldest daughter but a great-great-grandson of the third earl contested the will and claimed the earldom for himself and who was unfortunately already in possession of the ancestral seat of Kilkenny Castle. Thomas sought his brother-in-law's help in the dispute and the Duke of Norfolk raised the matter with the king who tried to settle the issue by arranging a marriage between James and Anne, therefore uniting the two claimants. For some reason the plan failed and James married elsewhere; it's unclear why negotiations failed as Henry himself wasn't interested in Anne as yet (and was involved in an affair with her older sister Mary around this time) but it could have been due to incompatibility or Thomas wanting the title for himself and a better marriage for his daughter.

Mary Boleyn had been recalled from France earlier than Anne, supposedly to end her affair with Francis I but also because a marriage had been arranged for her. In 1520, Mary married William Carey, a favourite courtier of Henry VIII who served as a Gentleman of the Privy Chamber; Henry himself attended the wedding. Soon after her marriage Mary became the king's mistress; however, due to Henry's discretion, we are unable to be entirely sure of the exact dates that they were involved. Mary would produce two children during her marriage to Carey, Catherine and Henry, and there is some debate as to whether the children were really her husband's or the king's.

Anne made her debut at the English court in a pageant titled the *Chateau Vert* which was held in honour of the imperial ambassadors; she appeared alongside her sister and future sister-in-law Jane Parker. The pageant portrayed the different virtues with the king's sister playing the part of Beauty, Mary Boleyn Kindness, Jane Constancy and Anne herself played Perseverance, an interesting foreshadow of things to come.[5] The pageant was a success and Anne quickly became one of the stars of the English court, attracting many admirers including the famous Tudor poet Sir Thomas Wyatt

One admirer was Henry Percy, the future Earl of Northumberland and it would seem the couple entered into an agreement or betrothal to marry each other before Cardinal Thomas Wolsey found out, who, in a fury, berated Percy in front of his household and then sent for his father who also berated him. The Ormond inheritance negotiations were not completely dead in the water at this time and Percy himself was betrothed to the daughter of the Earl of Shrewsbury, both potential matches that the king himself had a vested interest in. For Anne and Percy to think they could make their own arrangements infuriated their elders. The couple were forbidden to see each other and whilst Anne was sent back to Hever Castle, the Boleyn family seat, in disgrace, Percy was quickly married to his betrothed Mary Talbot. Anne always blamed Wolsey for the failure of this match and stated, 'If it ever lay in my power, I will work the Cardinal as much displeasure as he has done to me.'[6]

We can't be sure when exactly Henry became interested in Anne but most historians estimate it was early 1526. Henry probably expected a quick courtship and that a few gifts would encourage Anne to become his mistress but Anne, shockingly, refused. Anne had seen her sister used and discarded by the king and did not wish to suffer the same fate. Whilst Henry was unusually discreet in regards to his mistresses, he was not overly generous; his counterpart Francis I often showered his mistresses with gifts and allowed them a degree of influence both in public and private but Henry did not – even Bessie Blount who had provided him with the much-wanted proof he could have a son only received a respectable marriage and virtually disappeared from the records afterwards.

Anne skilfully maintained her refusal to be the king's mistress without offending or hurting his feelings, an impressive feat given the power the king had to make or break her family. She would often retreat to Hever Castle in order to put space between them but Henry started bombarding her with letters. Some of these letters survive in the Vatican Archives and whilst we don't have Anne's responses, we can clearly see the effect Anne was having on Henry. The letters are full of passion and love and confusion over Anne's behaviour, and one letter even shows the king reduced to schoolboy doodling: the initials AB are written enclosed by a heart and another letter is signed: 'H. no other A B seek R'.

Henry even offered to create the official and permanent post of the king's mistress for her but Anne refused again;[7] she had maintained her honour all these years and would not surrender it even for a king – she would only surrender it to her husband once she had one. She was smart and she knew her worth; she also knew that whatever Henry said, mistresses, even official ones, were sooner or later discarded and she did not want to ruin her own prospects nor did she want her children to be bastards, even royal ones. With this final refusal, Henry took the unprecedented step of offering Anne marriage.

Anne must have wondered how serious the king was as he had a wife and queen, one descended from blue blooded royalty no less. His queen had ties to some of the most powerful families in Europe, and she was also much loved by her people in England. Once Anne realised Henry was serious, she accepted – realistically, she had little choice. Whilst the court knew the king was interested in her, she would not receive a proposal from another man – it would be a 'career killer' for the brave soul who tried.

Once the couple had agreed to marry, they set about arranging the king's divorce from Catherine; they believed it would be a quick and simple matter. Henry instructed Wolsey to discreetly set up a legatine court and had himself 'summoned' to appear before it on the charge that he and Catherine had been living unlawfully together as Catherine had been his brother's wife and that therefore their marriage was unlawful and incestuous – and the proof was, they had no surviving sons; Princess Mary doesn't appear to have been considered at all. Henry always maintained this argument but was seemingly blind to the fact that the people around him were aware of his interest in Anne and were smart enough to realise that his scruples had suddenly appeared when she agreed to marry him. He would later go on to argue that he needed a son to succeed him and Catherine clearly could not provide one but we have to remember that Henry was more than willing for Anne to be his mistress in the beginning; it was her repeated refusals that pushed him to offer her marriage. The King's Great Matter came about firstly because Henry fell in love, closely followed by the fact he wanted and needed a son and he believed his new love could provide him with one.

As with most secrets, what Henry, Anne and Wolsey were up to was not secret for long. Catherine became aware days after the court opened of the proceedings against her and immediately notified her nephew, Emperor Charles V, who by strange coincidence had the Pope in his sway after the recent sack of Rome by his soldiers. The Pope's assent would be needed to enforce any decision any court made in regards to the Great Matter, so this was a bad start.

Both Henry and Anne seemed to disregard Catherine in their plans for the future. They seemed to believe she would do as she was told and that she would retire from the world and perhaps enter a convent. This would not have affected the legitimacy of the Princess Mary in any way, as during Tudor times, if a marriage was later found to be unlawful but had been entered into in 'good faith' by both parties, any children the couple had produced were still regarded as legitimate. However, Catherine was not willing to stand aside. She had been raised to believe her future and destiny was to be the Queen of England, she had fought for this destiny even after the death of her first husband. She had lived through years of uncertainty and poverty to become Henry's wife and queen and, most importantly of all, she did not regard their marriage as invalid – she always maintained that she had never had intercourse with Arthur and that in fact they had only shared a bed for seven or eight nights. Catherine was the daughter of Isabella of Castile, that glorious queen who with her husband, Ferdinand of Aragon, had united their countries and conquered Granada, ending Islamic rule and establishing Christianity as the dominant religion. She could trace her family history back through over a century of kings and queens from different countries and dynasties. Was this Infanta of Spain, a daughter of the 'Catholic Kings', the crowned and anointed Queen of England, going to step aside for a diplomat's daughter?

No.

Catherine learned that her husband was querying the legality of their marriage on the grounds that the dispensation that had been issued allowing the marriage in 1509, was faulty. The wording of the dispensation said that Catherine and Arthur's marriage had 'perhaps' been consummated and Wolsey believed this invalidated the entire document but Catherine had an ace up her sleeve. In Spain a brief had been issued at the same time as the dispensation which eliminated the difficulty caused by the word 'perhaps'; Catherine had a copy of it in her papers. Henry and Wolsey were entirely unaware of the existence of this brief and immediately ordered the royal archives to search for their own copy; when none was found, they suspected that the Spanish one was a forgery and demanded Catherine have the original sent from Spain. Catherine dutifully complied, writing to her nephew asking him to send the document to England, but secretly dispatched her physician with a separate message asking her nephew to keep hold of it – she had concerns that once it reached England, it would 'disappear': the brief never left Spain and only a notarised copy was ever seen by Henry and Wolsey.[8]

Catherine would struggle to have the case heard in Rome as she believed she would not receive impartial judgement in England, her husband's kingdom; Henry and Anne equally wanted the case to be decided in England as the Pope was in the emperor's power. After much debate and stalling the Pope eventually agreed to allow the case to be heard in England, dispatching Cardinal Campeggio to assist Wolsey in hearing the case. Campeggio had already offered his opinion that the marriage was good and valid; he was a reluctant judge, travelling as slowly as possible to England, and arriving in September 1528. He arrived in London on 8 December and whilst he awaited authorisation of his 'powers' to hold the court, he tried to persuade the king to abandon his plans for a divorce or persuade Catherine to allow her marriage to be annulled and enter a convent. Campeggio's incomplete powers were merely a stalling tactic and did him no favours as he failed miserably with both parties.

On 31 May 1529 Campeggio opened the Legatine Court at Blackfriars and in June issued summons for both the King and Queen of England to attend, a first in English royal history. The couple attended on 21 June, sitting on either side of the hall. The clerk of the court called out, 'King Henry of England, come into the court!' to which the king responded, 'Here my Lords!' The clerk then called out a second time, 'Catherine, Queen of England, come into the court!' Catherine did not respond; instead she rose from her seat and crossed the floor of the hall to her husband where she knelt before him and gave the speech of her life:[9]

Sir, I beseech you for all the loves that hath been between us, and for the love of God, let me have justice and right, take of me some pity and compassion, for I am a poor woman and a stranger born out of your dominion, I have here no assured friend, and much less indifferent counsel: I flee to you as to the head of justice within this realm,

Alas! Sir, wherein have I offended you, or what occasion of displeasure have I designed against your will and pleasure? Intending (as I perceive) to put me from you, I take God and all the world to witness, that I have been to you a true and humble wife, ever conformable to your will and pleasure, that never said or did anything to the contrary thereof, being always well pleased and contented with all things wherein ye had any delight or dalliance, whether it were in little or much, I never grudged in word or countenance, or showed a visage or spark of discontentation. I loved all those whom ye loved only for your sake, whether I had cause or no; and whether they were my friends or my enemies.

This twenty years I have been your true wife or more, and by me ye have had divers children, although it hath pleased God to call them out of this world, which hath been no default in me.

And when ye had me at the first, I take God to be my judge, I was a true maid without touch of man. And whether it be true or no, I put it to your conscience. If there be any just cause by the law that ye can allege against me, either of dishonesty or any other impediment to banish and put me from you, I am well content to depart, to my great shame and dishonour; and if there be none, then here I most lowly beseech you let me remain in my former estate, and receive justice at your princely hand.

The king, your father, was in the time of his reign of such estimation through the world for his excellent wisdom, that he was accounted and called of all men the second Solomon; and my father Ferdinand, King of Spain, who was esteemed to be one of the wittiest princes that reigned in Spain many years before, were both wise and excellent kings in wisdom and princely behaviour. It is not therefore to be doubted, but that they were elected and gathered as wise counsellors about them as to their high discretions was thought meet.

Also, as me seemeth there was in those days as wise, as well-learned men, and men of good judgement as be present in both realms, who thought then the marriage between you and me good and lawful. Therefore, is it a wonder to me what new inventions are now invented against me, that never intended but honesty. And cause me to stand to the order and judgment of this new court, wherein ye may do me much wrong, if ye intend any cruelty; for ye may condemn me for lack of sufficient answer, having no indifferent counsel, but such as be assigned me, with whose wisdom and learning I am not acquainted. Ye must consider that they cannot be indifferent counsellors for my part which be your subjects, and taken out of your own council before, wherein they be made privy, and dare not, for your displeasure, disobey your will and intent, being once made privy thereto.

Therefore, I most humbly require you, in the way of charity, and for the love of God, who is the just judge, to spare the extremity of this new court, until I may be advertised what way and order my friends in Spain will advise me to take. And if ye will not extend to me so much indifferent favour, your pleasure then be fulfilled, and to God I commit my case![10]

Catherine of Aragon pleads her case against divorce from Henry VIII by Henry Nelson O'Neil, nineteenth century. It's not known if Jane witnessed Catherine's passionate plea in person but like others, she would have soon heard of it.

Henry had tried to raise Catherine but she refused to move; with the eyes of the court on him and knowing they were sympathetic to his wife, he was forced to agree to her request to appeal to Rome. Catherine then rose, curtsied to her husband and turned to depart on the arm of Master Griffith, her general receiver, ignoring the court crier shouting 'Catherine Queen of England, come into the Court'. When Master Griffith tentatively pointed out they were asking her to return, Catherine responded, 'On, on, it maketh no matter, for it is no indifferent court for me, therefore I will not tarry; go on your ways.' She would never return.

By the end of July Campeggio had adjourned the case and referred it back to Rome; Henry and Anne were furious. It was the beginning of the end for Wolsey. For Catherine it was a victory but it would turn out to be a hollow one: she had got what she wanted, the case referred to Rome, but there was no judgement either way. Henry had not changed his mind and was still determined to annul their marriage.

Chapter 5

Cinderella

Anyone who supported and loved Catherine would have been impressed with her stand at Blackfriars and Jane would have been no exception. Jane quickly came to admire and love her mistress which explains her later behaviour towards Anne Boleyn. Anne was always unfairly blamed for the breakdown of the royal marriage despite it being the king who initiated everything. Then as now people formed their own opinions on what they believed and this situation was no exception: this was a time when a king could do no wrong and you didn't criticise him as God's representative on earth; this was how it became so easy to scapegoat 'the other woman'. Others seemed to be aware of what was really going on, despite Henry's claims to the contrary, but they were forced to hold their tongues. Which category did Jane fall in? Catherine herself always believed if Anne was removed from Henry's side, she would be able to bring the king back to her, and perhaps Jane, thanks to her proximity to the queen, was influenced by this thinking? She had also been raised by her family in obedience and loyalty to the king and may have genuinely believed he had been led astray. Jane's true thoughts will never be known and there was nothing she

Cardinal Thomas Wolsey, artist and year unknown. His failure to end Henry's marriage to Catherine of Aragon cost him his position at court and lost him Henry's favour.

could have done anyway, but her sympathies always lay with Catherine and her daughter.

After the failure of Blackfriars, the court returned to existing in an uneasy and tense atmosphere, Catherine was still the queen, Henry was still married to her and Anne was still the king's love but there was one massive change: Cardinal Wolsey was stripped of his position as Chancellor and forced to surrender all his possessions, including the magnificent Hampton Court Palace. Henry and Anne blamed him for the failure at Blackfriars and Anne became convinced the cardinal was doing everything to stop her marriage. By coincidence Catherine herself was also angry with the cardinal as she believed the doubts over her marriage had sprung from him, and both women had worked (separately) to distance Henry from him.

Wolsey was allowed to retain his position as Archbishop of York and travelled for the first time to his diocese in 1530 where a few months later he was accused of treason and ordered back to London to stand trial, but he became ill on the journey and, perhaps mercifully, died at Leicester on 29 November 1530. Just before his death he reportedly said: 'I see the matter against me how it is framed. But if I had served God as diligently as I have done the king, he would not have given me over in my grey hairs.'[1]

Wolsey's removal and death paved the way for Thomas Cromwell to take his place and for the King's Great Matter to move towards its conclusion. For a short time, the king and queen continued to keep up appearances, attending court functions and sharing private dinners with each other; they also talked of their daughter but the cracks were growing wider until finally, in July 1531, Henry and Anne left Catherine at Windsor Castle without notification: Catherine would never see Henry again. Jane would have witnessed the surprise and confusion this incident caused and would have begun to feel the doubt creeping in as the king did not reappear. Speculation was rife but finally Catherine's abandonment was confirmed when she sent the king a letter asking after him for clarification. He angrily responded that he had no need to bid her farewell and insisted she stop sending him letters, and when she tried once more, it was retorted that 'she would do more wisely to employ her time in seeking witnesses to prove her pretended virginity, than to waste it in holding such language to all the world as she did; and instead of writing to him, or sending messages, she had better attend to her own affairs'.[2]

Catherine was ordered to leave Windsor with her household and retire to the More in Hertfordshire; she resisted this forced exile until November before departing for what she described as 'one of the worst houses in England'.[3] Her daughter was ordered to Richmond; they would never see each other again. No changes had been made to Catherine's servants or status as queen as yet; she still had around 200 servants in attendance and there is no reason to suspect Jane wasn't with her but this was a very difficult time. They were cut off from court and news trickled through slowly; all they could do was carry on as normal as best as they could and wait. Catherine's servants continued to serve her as queen as revealed by a rare visit she received at the More by two Venetian diplomats who witnessed her dining whilst surrounded by her maids of honour and served by her ladies. This state of affairs couldn't continue and after being moved to a better accommodation at Ampthill, Bedfordshire, but still far from court, Catherine received the horrifying news that destroyed her world: her husband had married Anne Boleyn.

The blow was delivered by the dukes of Suffolk and Norfolk and was received by Catherine and her assembled household in disbelief.[4] There had been no word from Rome or the Pope but the dukes explained that Henry had broken with Rome and was now recognised as the head of the Church in England. Worse was to follow: Anne Boleyn was pregnant and she and her supporters were confident the child would be a boy.

Jane would have borne witness to Catherine's horror and heartbreak. She may also have been confused and frightened herself. How could the king break with the Church? All sorts of thoughts must have run through her head. What did

Thomas Cranmer, Archbishop of Canterbury, by an unknown artist. The portrait is almost certainly posthumous, seventeenth century onwards. Along with the dukes of Suffolk and Norfolk, he was godfather to Edward and aided his godson in making reforms in the Church of England.

it mean? What would happen now? Would Catherine be exiled even further from the court? Would she require as many servants? Did she still have a place in her household? Would she be forced to leave her side?

Some of the answers came quickly: Catherine was told she was no longer to call herself the queen but the Princess Dowager, a title she was entitled to as the widow of Prince Arthur; and the king would not provide for her personal expenses or her servants in future. She was to have a small allowance which automatically implied the downsizing of her household and activities in future. Soon after, she received a summons from the new Archbishop of Canterbury Thomas Cranmer, to attend a court at Dunstable to determine the validity of her marriage, but she refused. The court proceeded without her and the archbishop found that her marriage had been invalid from the beginning as the Pope's power did not include allowing the marriage of a brother and sister-in-law; Catherine, awaiting the outcome of her case in Rome, ignored him.

In August 1533, she was ordered to remove herself and her household to Buckden, another remote residence, and was informed that Henry was providing her with an allowance of 12,000 crowns to maintain her household. When everything was organised, Catherine was left with a much reduced household, of those she only trusted her apothecary, physician, her confessor and only ten ladies, quite a significant reduction from a household of two hundred.

Jane was not one of the ladies who travelled to Buckden; she may have felt a mixed bag of emotions including relief and despair as she would not share her mistress's exile and diminish her prospects – but she would have to part from a woman she had grown to admire and care for. The question was, what was Jane to do now? We know she went on to serve Anne Boleyn but it is not clear when she was appointed to do so. A 'Mrs Seymour' received a New Year's gift from the king in 1534 that some have taken as proof that Jane entered Queen Anne's service not long after leaving Catherine's; however, 'Mrs Seymour' could also be Jane's future close friend and sister-in-law, Anne Stanhope, who had married her brother Edward by this time. It was common in the sixteenth century to refer to both married and single women as 'Mrs', adding to the confusion surrounding the identity of the 'Mrs Seymour' of 1534.[5]

The facts are that Anne's household had already been formed whilst Jane was still serving Catherine so there may have been no place for her at the time. It is probable she returned to Wolf Hall to await her family's decision on a suitable next step where she must have wondered what the future held for her.

The exact date Henry married his second wife is unknown but two dates have been given weight by contemporary records: 14 November 1532[6] and 28 January 1533.[7] It is easy to see why Henry and Anne were discreet as both of these dates fell within the time Catherine was still considered by England and the world to be Henry's wife and queen; there had been no verdict from Rome or announcement from the English government. The November date comes from the chronicler Edward Hall who wrote: 'The King, after his return [from Calais] married privily the Lady Anne Boleyn on St Erkenwald's Day, which marriage was kept so secret, that very few knew it, 'til she was great with child, at Easter after.'[8]

Henry and Anne had travelled to France in the summer of 1532 to gain the support of Francis I for their marriage. They had reason to be hopeful: Anne had served at the French court and Francis had an even more difficult relationship with the emperor than Henry did. Charles ruled vast swathes of territory including Spain, Austria and a number of smaller areas neighbouring France, making him a constant thorn in the side of the French king. One of the low points came when Francis was captured by men leading Charles's forces and imprisoned in Madrid where he was forced to sign a treaty which involved large and humiliating concessions to Charles regarding the status of Burgundy and Francis's claims to Naples and Milan; he was even required to marry Charles's elder sister Eleanor. The second low point came when he was required to hand over his two sons in order to secure his freedom, which he reluctantly did but the minute he was free, he renounced all the promises and agreements he had made as they had been made under duress. All this history could work in the couple's favour.

Before they left England, Henry created Anne the Marquess of Pembroke, making her a high-ranking peeress in her own right and of suitable rank to be presented to Europe as the future Queen of England. A demand was made of Catherine to return the queen's jewels for Anne's use to which Catherine strongly resisted, famously declaring she would not resign them to adorn one who was considered 'the scandal of Christendom'; she was forced to give in.[9]

A new problem presented itself when no suitable royal or noble woman could be found to receive Anne. Henry refused to meet Francis's wife,

Queen Eleanor, the niece of Catherine of Aragon; equally, Queen Eleanor had no interest in meeting the woman trying to replace her aunt. Marguerite of Navarre would also not greet Anne much to her horror. Francis eventually suggested his mistress, Anne de Pisseleu d'Heilly, Duchess d'Étampes, who was regarded by Henry as unsuitable as Anne was to be his wife not his mistress. In the end the kings agreed to meet in Boulogne without the ladies present. What followed was nearly a month of feasting and talks as the two kings tried to outdo each other in their magnificence, before Henry escorted Francis to Calais to greet Anne; it was two days before she appeared before him disguised in a masque on 27 October and boldly asked the French king to dance. Henry and Anne both thought the meeting a success but it would later become apparent that Francis would put his own interests first, understandably so. After a delay caused by bad weather, the couple set sail for England, landing in Dover two days later and, according to Hall, they were married on 14 November.

The second date, 25 January 1533, is hypothesized as being after the couple finally consummated their relationship following their successful visit to France and Anne began to suspect she was pregnant. Any baby Anne was carrying had to be legitimate as the future heir to the throne so a ceremony in January was quietly arranged and performed to ensure this, but could both dates be correct? Perhaps Henry and Anne underwent some sort of ceremony in November before they reaffirmed their relationship in a second ceremony in January.

Claire Ridgway from the Anne Boleyn Files has written extensively

Jane Seymour copied by Francesco Bartolozzi and published by John Chamberlaine, c. 1792.

on Anne and believes the former date to be correct as the couple started living together as man and wife at this time and Anne fell pregnant shortly after.

Jane remained at Wolf Hall, only hearing about events at court from a distance. Her brother Edward will have written back to his family to keep them informed of news as he learnt it. Jane will have whiled away the time helping her mother and looking after her younger siblings; everyone had a part to play in a Tudor household.

On 7 September 1533 Queen Anne gave birth to a healthy child but it was not the son Henry had been hoping for but another daughter; they would call her Elizabeth after both of their mothers. The couple were disappointed but pleased that Anne had proved she could have healthy children – they knew they had to put on a brave face as the rest of the world was watching: after all Henry had done to provide a son and heir, he had produced another daughter.

What did Jane feel when she learned that Anne had produced a daughter? I imagine she felt a degree of triumph on Catherine and Mary's behalf: the 'other woman' hadn't produced a son either. Perhaps in thoughts she would have kept to herself she believed that this would be a sign to the king that God did not approve of his actions. She would later see God's Hand in the Pilgrimage of Grace. Perhaps she felt worried. Jane has been credited with good sense and calm understanding and had seen the king set Catherine aside in order to produce a son only for his new love not to do so. All the changes that were appearing in England had been brought about for the purpose of a son and heir and Anne hadn't delivered. Was it all for nothing? What would happen now? These anxious thoughts will have been displaced by news of a potential match for her with the son and heir of the Dormer family.[10]

The Dormers were successful wool merchants based in Buckinghamshire, close enough to the Seymours' family home for Jane to have knowledge of them. The head of the family was Sir Robert Dormer of West Wycombe and Wing; he had married Jane Newdigate of Harefield, Middlesex, and sometime before 1514 they had produced their only child, a son, Sir William Dormer. It's possible that the Seymours' old friend Sir Francis Bryan started the negotiations for the match but it is equally possible Jane's father or brother did.

Whoever approached the Dormers failed in their mission on Jane's behalf. Two reasons have been suggested for this. The first is that Lady Dormer did not think Jane was a good enough match for her only son. As we have previously seen, Jane was one of a large family; her father would have to have been careful with dowries and lands for his daughters and perhaps he could not make a decent enough offer in Lady Dormer's eyes. Or perhaps there was something else in connection to Jane's father. A scandal?

It is often forgotten that Edward Seymour was actually married twice. The wife everyone remembers is Anne Stanhope but she was his second wife; his first wife was Catherine Fillol, daughter of Sir William Fillol of Woodlands, Horton, Dorset, and of Fillol's Hall, Essex. She was also his co-heiress.[11] It has been alleged that Catherine had had an affair with her father-in-law, Sir John Seymour; the rumours spread far enough to be known at court. Whilst there is no surviving evidence, a seventeenth-century marginal note in a copy of Vincent's *Baronage* at the College of Heralds mentions this rumour.

Whatever really happened entirely destroyed Catherine and Edward's marriage, her relationship with her father and Edward's relationship with his father-in-law. Catherine was forced to enter a convent and Sir William later wrote in his will: 'for many diverse causes and considerations, neither Catherine nor her heirs of her body, nor Sir Edward Seymour her husband in any wise were [are] to inherit any part or parcel of his lands.' He left his daughter only £40 on condition that 'she shall live virtuously and abide in some house of religion of women'.[12]

It is not overstating the situation to say this was catastrophic. Families jealously controlled their wealth and lands and often went to great efforts to ensure they remained in the family. There are no records of Catherine having siblings so she should have inherited (and by extension Edward) everything on her father's death. It is interesting to note that Sir William did not want Edward to inherit anything either. Did he know something we don't? Did he blame Edward for the affair? Edward would later challenge the will in 1531, claiming that his father-in-law was not of sound mind when he wrote it; it is unclear if this is also true. Edward never divorced Catherine but he had remarried by March 1535, thereby implying that Catherine had died by this point. She left two sons, John and Edward, but their father made sure only the children he had with his second wife could inherit his land and titles, and only if this line died out were the descendants of Catherine to inherit. John never married but Edward did and he had a son. In 1750, the 7th Duke of Somerset, Algernon Seymour, died; his son predeceased him. Anne and Edward's line had ended and the present Duke of Somerset is descended from Catherine Fillol.

If the court had heard rumours of the scandal, then Lady Dormer would have too and she would not have wanted her only child to be attached to a family mired in scandal. The second reason for the failed negotiations is Sir Francis Bryan himself. Whilst proving himself a good friend to the Seymours, he had a bit of a reputation as a ladies' man and for a lack of scruples which eventually earned him the nickname 'the Vicar of Hell'. Again, it is Lady Dormer who is unhappy with the match: 'detesting the conditions of this knight [Francis] she played along while her husband and Francis were discussing the match, and then took her son off to the Sidneys, where she arranged a marriage with their daughter'.[13] Whichever reason it was, it appears that Lady Dormer held nothing against Jane herself, but there was an implied swipe later on:

> For when Lady Dormer saw the corruption of the state of the kingdom, her desire was to marry her son with some virtuous gentlewoman, answerable in quality. The Lady Dormer in this prudent and valorous act, to have her son matched in a kindred of good fame, that neither the power of so great a favourite nor the gaining of so mighty a friend at court, could move this lady to marry her son with Bryan's niece who had made shipwreck of his Faith and honesty.[14]

This account comes from William's daughter Jane, Duchess of Feria, who may have been told it as a family legend. It's also possible she learned of it from her mistress, Mary I, who may have heard about it at the time or possibly from Jane herself, though whether Jane would take the risk of talking about a prior potential betrothal at the time she was married to the king is dicey to say the least, especially with what happened to Anne Boleyn. We will never know but the fact that these two women had something in common in relation to Jane Seymour may have encouraged a sharing of confidences and an exchange of stories.

Did William court Jane? If he did there is no surviving evidence; what is clear is that they were never properly betrothed. When Henry's interest in Jane became apparent, this prior potential match never became an issue, unlike an undetermined relationship Anne Boleyn had with Henry Percy prior to her marriage to the king. William would eventually marry twice and neither one of his marriages was ever accused of having an impediment. Jane emerged from this negotiation with her reputation intact and in fact would go on to be considered in some histories as a 'Cinderella' who was jilted and then went on to marry a more prestigious man.

Portrait of an unknown lady, said to be Jane Dormer, Duchess of Feria by Antonis Mor, c. 1558. Jane was a daughter of Sir William Dormer who was once a potential husband to Jane Seymour but the plans fell through. Possibly named after the queen for sentimental or practical reasons, she would go on to become a friend of Jane's son Edward and her stepdaughter Mary.

William lived a long life and had many children, dying in 1575, aged about 72. It is interesting to speculate on this episode from Jane's life. What were her feelings towards William and his to her? Were there any? Did William think about the woman he almost married who then became England's queen? Did Jane think how different life would have been if she had married him? William did have a daughter he named Jane. Was this in honour of his mother, a much loved queen who died too soon or in honour of a lost love?

By strange coincidence, Jane Dormer would later be a playmate of Jane's only son Prince Edward and a surviving tale has the two playing cards and Edward saying; 'Now Jane, your king is gone. I shall be good enough for you.'[15]

Chapter 6

Catching the King's Eye

By 1535 Jane had returned to court. After the failure of the Dormer match, Sir Francis Bryan had used his connections to the Boleyns and got her a place in the Queen's Household. This would have been an interesting situation: on one hand she was returning to court where she would have a second chance to progress and make a good marriage, and she was also back at the centre of events and would not have to rely on third-hand news.

The downside was the queen was Anne and not Catherine. Catherine and Anne ran vastly different households; whilst they both had a sincere interest in learning and culture and both believed and sincerely promoted piety, Anne was for reform and Catherine was for the old ways; Jane was also for the old ways. Anne's household was also a livelier place, and whilst the court was always filled with banquets, entertainment and masques, historians have noted that the entertainments at Henry's court reached their peak during Anne Boleyn's queenship. Jane's natural shyness and reserved demeanour may have made the new, 'hectic' court difficult to navigate at first but she soon grew and adapted.

She would have soon realised that things were not all well between the royal couple; Anne had still not produced a son. A handful of evidence survives to indicate that Anne was pregnant in 1534 but nothing more is recorded beyond that and to make

A French eighteenth-century engraving of Jane Seymour, artist unknown.

matter worse Henrys eye had started wandering quite soon after their marriage. Unlike Catherine who had rarely remonstrated with her husband, Anne could not turn a blind eye to his flirtations and berated him for his behaviour. This was not something Henry was used to or prepared to tolerate from any woman, telling Anne 'that she must shut her eyes, and endure as well as more worthy persons, and that she ought to know that it was in his power to humble her again in a moment more than he had exalted her'.[1]

Once Anne became Henry's wife, she was expected to adopt a subservient role but Anne was used to being an equal player in the relationship and found the change difficult. Another factor working against her was that her marriage had been based primarily on love and infatuation unlike other royal marriages of time. If Anne lost Henry's love, she had very little to fall back on to preserve their marriage, Catherine was a blue-blooded princess from a powerful foreign country and she had been set aside, so what chance did Anne have without Henry? Catherine's royal background protected her from the worst of Henry's threats and recriminations when she refused to comply, Anne did not have this protection.

The women who briefly caught Henry's eye during his marriage to Anne largely remain unknown but there has been speculation that the lady known as the 'Imperial Lady' was in fact Jane herself. I, however, don't believe this is the case. The unidentified woman obviously supported Catherine and the Princess Mary and she may even have been known to Jane, but Chapuys, who watched events with a keen interest, never made the connection when Jane herself later came to prominence, something he surely would have done as it is thanks to one of his dispatches that we are aware of the 'Imperial Lady's' existence:

> Renewed and increased the love he formerly had for a very beautiful damsel of the court; and because the said lady [Anne] wished to drive her away, the king has been very angry, telling his said lady that she had good reason to be content with what he had done for her, which he would not do now if the thing were to begin, and that she should consider from what she had come and several other things.[2]

He never described Jane as beautiful either.

Was Jane brought to the court to be the king's mistress? At this point I think not. Any woman at court was a possible mistress and Jane was one woman amongst many at the time who, without being disrespectful, could get lost in the crowd. Whilst clearly wanting to progress, she did not push herself forward and become the centre of attention like Anne had done; instead, she quietly watched what was going on around her and waited for an opportunity to present itself; perhaps this trait is why she was later reported to be a skilled huntress who never missed the hunt.

Jane stars in a short video at Hampton Court Palace telling the story of Henry VIII and his six wives. (*Author's collection*)

Circumstances would soon bring the possibility into focus however. In the autumn of 1535, Henry set off on his annual Progress and on 3 September arrived at Wolf Hall.[3] Some have questioned whether Jane was present for this visit but as it was her family home, it is unthinkable that she wasn't there; she may have arrived as part of the Queen's Household or she may have been given leave to help prepare for the king's visit – each theory is equally plausible.

Was it at this time Jane first came to Henry's attention? All historians agree that Henry had charm and approachability; yes, it did decrease as he aged and his temper worsened, but when he so chose, he had the gift of the personal touch and, as a daughter of the family he was currently staying with, he would have shown every member of the family courtesy and respect. I believe this was the first time Henry 'saw' Jane. There is no denying he would have seen her at court of course; as a lady to both his queens, he would have at least seen or known her in passing but I believe this was the first time he became directly aware of her. In her

✠ BOUND TO OBEY AND SERVE ✠

JANE SEYMOUR
DIED
c1508 — 1537

Henry VIII's third wife, Jane Seymour, was very different to Anne Boleyn, both in looks and character. Apparently meek and obedient, she was described as being '*of middle stature and no great beauty, so fair that one would call her rather pale than otherwise.*' Hans Holbein completed this portrait in 1536; it is considered a good likeness.

DIED

A portrait of Jane greets you as you enter the Great Watching Chamber at Hampton Court Palace. (*Author's Collection*)

home environment, a place she knew well, Jane's usual reserve would have relaxed slightly and she would have flourished, and perhaps a certain degree of confidence made itself known which Henry recognised. The court stayed at Wolf Hall for a few days, during which time it would have been quite literally all hands on deck, while Henry would have had an opportunity to see Jane in a new light – assisting her mother, perhaps instructing the household staff and caring for her younger siblings; perhaps she hunted with the royal party or escorted them around the gardens known as 'the Great paled garden', 'My Old Lady's Garden' and 'My Young Lady's Garden'.[4] Whatever brought Jane to Henry's attention, she remained in his thoughts on his departure, and she would never really leave them.

The Progress ended with the king and queen returning to Windsor Castle at the end of October; it appears to have been successful. Henry and Anne had been able show themselves to the people with little sign of trouble and had worked to drum up support for the new queen and reform of the Church.[5] At some point Henry and Anne reconciled, with the result that she fell pregnant; perhaps being away from the capital had eased pressures on them. The court was aware of the pregnancy by Christmas.

What did this mean for Jane? At the time very little, for her personally anyway. The Queen of England was pregnant again, her child could be the son and heir Henry and England were waiting for; if so, Anne's position would be secure.[6] The people would have no recourse to argue against Henry's new marriage as God would have shown his favour.

We don't know if Jane was aware of the king's interest until he directly, or indirectly, made her aware. In the past, when his wife was 'unavailable' to him, Henry had usually taken a mistress and during the last months of 1535, Jane was the woman he chose for the honour. He doesn't appear to have been very original in his approach, though he may have thought that if it had worked once, then why not again. In the early stages of their courtship Henry had gifted Anne his portrait in a bracelet and he gave a similar gift to Jane but in a necklace. A gift from the king was a sign of favour but a gift to a woman could also be taken as a sign of romantic affection; it certainly started the gossip.

Jane must have been surprised to receive this gift, surprised but pleased. It's quite possible she had never before received a gift from a man unrelated to her – we don't know if William Dormer had sent her gifts during their short-lived betrothal. The necklace would not have been cheap either; we know that Henry didn't do anything by halves – it would have been valuable and beautiful. This was a new opportunity but what did it mean? Was the king interested in her as his mistress? Was he simply being bountiful? It was part of the role of a king after all. One person who was quite sure where this was leading was the queen herself. Anne soon heard of the rumours surrounding her husband and Jane and in one incident apparently tore the necklace from Jane's neck:

> It is currently traditional that at her first coming to court, Queen Anne Boleyn, espying a jewel pendant about her neck, snatched thereat, (desirous to see, the other unwilling to show it) and casually hurt her hand with her own violence; but it grieved her heart more, when she perceived it the king's picture by himself bestowed up on her, who from this day forward dated her own declining and the others ascending, in her husband's affection.[7]

This interpretation was not strictly true in 1535; this excerpt is from Thomas Fuller's *History of the Worthies of England* which was published in the seventeenth century, wherein Fuller had the benefit of hindsight and knew what happened next. From the point of view of the court at the time, yes, the king and queen had been going through a rough patch but they had been noted to have lovers' quarrels before; also Anne was pregnant, and the harsh truth was that the marriage could survive without as much affection as had previously been the case – a lot of marriages, especially royal marriages, did. Kings took mistresses all the time; it was practically expected and they had never been a threat to the queen before.

The problem Anne had was that her marriage proved that a queen could be set aside for a mistress; hers was based primarily on love and her ability to give Henry a son, both of which were on shaky ground by the end of 1535. As she couldn't predict the result of her pregnancy, she had to try to control whom Henry set his eye on instead and hopefully keep one threat at bay.

There was another threat she possibly didn't foresee at the time but may have realised later: Catherine of Aragon was dying. The former queen had been ill for a number of weeks, but news reached the court in

January 1536 that this would be her last illness.[8] Catherine's last home was at Kimbolton Castle in Cambridgeshire, and whilst it was in better condition than some of the other houses where she had been exiled, it was still a marked come-down from her previous residences. Her household was completely depleted as well, though this was partially her choice; she refused to interact with anyone who did not recognise her as queen and kept her distance from the servants Henry had provided for her as she did not trust them and regarded them as her jailors. She surrounded herself with the last handful of trusted servants and ladies she had, as well as her Spanish confessor, apothecary and doctor.

The Imperial Ambassador, Eustace Chapuys, was finally given permission to visit and was horrified to find her much changed from the woman he had last seen five years before and realised she didn't have long left; she was so weak she had taken to her bed. Catherine was delighted to see her old friend and ally stating, 'Now I can die in your arms, not abandoned like one of the beasts.' He stayed for four days and in that time succeeded in cheering her up, making her laugh and perhaps talking of home or better times. Catherine received one final surprise in the form of Maria de Salinas, one of her oldest friends and former lady in waiting.[9] It's possible Maria had travelled to England with Catherine; if she hadn't, she arrived shortly after her and remained in England for the rest of her life. Maria had heard of her former mistress's impending end and had begged to be allowed to see her but was refused by the king, so, ignoring him, she had travelled alone to Kimbolton. It was not an easy journey to make and Maria suffered a fall from her horse on the way, something she used to her advantage when she finally arrived looking bedraggled and covered in mud. She told Sir Edmund Bedingfield, Catherine's chief steward (appointed by Henry) that she had a permit from the king but had lost it when she fell and that her servants were currently looking for it. Bedingfield fell for the ploy and allowed Maria inside where she disappeared into Catherine's chambers and never came back out. Soon after realising what had happened, Bedingfield rather sheepishly had to admit to Cromwell: 'Since that time, we never saw her, neither any letters of her licence hither to repair.'[10]

During her final hours it is believed Catherine dictated one last letter to the man she still regarded, and loved, as her husband:

My most dear lord, King and husband,

The hour of my death now drawing on, the tender love I ouge [owe] thou forceth me, my case being such, to commend myselv to thou, and to put thou in remembrance with a few words of the healthe and safeguard of thine allm [soul] which thou ougte to preferce before all worldley matters, and before the care and pampering of thy body, for the which thoust have cast me into many calamities and thineselv into many troubles. For my part, I pardon thou everything, and I desire to devoutly pray God that He will pardon thou also. For the rest, I commend unto thou our doughtere Mary, beseeching thou to be a good father unto her, as I have heretofore desired. I entreat thou also, on behalve of my maides, to give them marriage portions, which is not much, they being but three. For all mine other servants I solicit the wages due them, and a year more, lest they be unprovided for. Lastly, I makest this vouge [vow], that mine eyes desire thou aboufe all things. Katharine the Quene.[11]

Defiant until the end, she signed herself 'Katharine the Quene', the title she believed she was rightly entitled too. Shortly after Catherine of Aragon, former Infanta of Spain and Queen of England for twenty-four years, died peacefully in the arms of her old friend Maria on 7 January 1536; she was 50.

The news quickly reached Henry and Anne; Anne rewarded the messenger with a handsome present, and in a rather distasteful display both king and queen reacted joyously and with the court erupted into celebration. Chapuys wrote to Charles V:

You could not conceive the joy that the King and those who favour this concubinage have shown at the death of the good queen, especially the Earl of Wiltshire and his son [Anne Boleyn's father and brother], who said it was a pity that the Princess [Mary] did not keep company with her. The King, on the Saturday he heard the news exclaimed 'God be praised that we are free from all suspicion of war'; and that the time had come that he would manage the French better than he had done hitherto, because they would do now whatever he wanted from a fear lest he should ally himself again with your majesty, seeing that the cause which disturbed your friendship was gone. On the following day, Sunday, the King was clad all over in yellow, from top to toe except the white feather he had in his bonnet, and the Little Bastard [Elizabeth] was conducted to mass with trumpets and other great triumphs. After dinner the King entered the room in which the ladies danced, and there did several things like one transported with joy. At last, he sent for his Little Bastard, and carrying her in his arms he showed her first to one and then to another.[12]

The celebrations would continue for days but it was recorded that in private Anne was more subdued.[13] Yes, she was now the only queen of England but in a strange way Catherine had also been Anne's protection. Whilst she lived, if for whatever reason Henry might try to set her aside, he would have immediately been expected to return to Catherine. Whilst it had been difficult to have one ex-wife living, having two would have been nigh on impossible and would have made him the laughing stock of Europe. Any potential third marriage he contemplated would be even more doubtful than his controversial second. It is not unreasonable to say that Catherine's continued existence was an unconventional, and sometimes unrealised, prop to his second marriage. As Annette Crosbie's Catherine of Aragon stated in *The Six Wives of Henry VIII* TV series of 1970, 'Whilst I am alive, she is safe'.

Jane's reaction on hearing the news of Catherine's death is not recorded but can be imagined: she had loved and respected the Spanish queen and would have been sickened by the celebrations taking place around her. During it all, I think she would have made time to say a prayer for her former mistress and mourned her quietly; her thoughts might have turned to her daughter Mary and how she was coping. It's not known who broke the news to Mary and how sensitively it was done but her reaction could not have been in doubt to anyone who knew her: she was devastated. Shortly after Catherine's death, probably due to a combination of stress and grief, she fell seriously ill and it was thought her life was in danger for a time but she did recover.

Anne, whether wisely or foolishly, wrote in the same month to try to reconcile with her stepdaughter, telling her that if she submitted to her father's laws, she would be welcomed back to court and would be exempt from carrying the queen's train and even walk beside her, but Mary flatly refused.[14] It does appear to show a lack of sensitivity on Anne's part to approach a young girl who was mired in grief following the loss of her beloved mother and who may have held her responsible for her death; a degree of tact should have been used but realistically, even had Anne waited a month or so, Mary would never have reconciled with her. In Anne's defence perhaps she was trying to secure more support or close off another avenue of danger, but either way it was doomed to failure.

On 24 January 1536 Henry took part in a celebratory joust but was thrown from his horse and knocked unconscious for over two hours. Had he died that day there might have been civil war. There were four possible claimants to the throne at the time: officially Princess Elizabeth was the legal heir to the throne but she was only 3 years old and the child of a controversial marriage; then there was her elder sister Mary who had been, and still was, regarded as legitimate by more than half the country since her birth, and who was older at 19 – but both were female. The third claimant was Henry Fitzroy, Duke of Richmond, who was 16 and had been illegitimate from birth but was male, always a deciding factor in Tudor politics. The fourth and last claimant was Queen Anne's unborn baby and there was no guarantee of sex or even the baby being born alive. There was also the timeframe to consider: it's not known exactly how far along Anne was in her pregnancy but the first recorded mentions of it were towards the end of 1535. Later, when disaster struck, the Imperial Ambassador and others wrote she was around three and a half months pregnant so that gives us an estimated expected birthdate of July/August 1536, which meant that England would have had no definite ruler for six or seven months, an impossible circumstance.

Thankfully, Henry regained consciousness and the situation was avoided but Henry, his councillors and his people would not have been unaware of what had just nearly happened. Anne herself was brought the news of Henry's accident by her uncle and there are conflicting sources of how it was told to her: one states sensitively and the other bluntly. From surviving evidence of the Duke of Norfolk's personality it is perhaps easy to believe the latter; however, he must have been aware of his niece's condition and how important this pregnancy was. Nevertheless, Henry appeared to be well and Anne and the court could settle down and wait for her pregnancy to progress.

Catherine of Aragon's funeral was held at Peterborough Abbey (now Cathedral) on 29 January 1536 and it was there she was laid to rest; the funeral was not for a queen but for a princess dowager and one of the reasons her old friend and ally Chapuys refused to attend. The sermon was preached by John Hilsey, Bishop of Rochester, who disgraced himself by saying that at the end Catherine had acknowledged that she had never been Queen of England, a blatant lie that no one in the congregation believed.[15] To Henry's credit he wore black the day of Catherine's interment and attended a mass in her honour but Anne reportedly wore yellow again and complained that all anyone spoke about was the good end her rival had made.

Jane would have witnessed Anne's celebration and Henry's mourning and mourned privately herself; perhaps she prayed for her. She would have felt a mixture of sadness and comfort as Catherine was beyond all pain now and no doubt with God but there was no turning back the clock: she was gone and Anne remained queen.

What happened next may have been seen by Jane and the pro-Catherine party as her revenge from beyond the grave or the Lord's doing, as on the day of her funeral Anne went into premature labour and suffered a miscarriage; according to Chapuys and the chronicler Charles Wriothesley, the child was developed enough to be recognised as a boy. In a letter to his master dated 10 February, Chapuys explained:

> On the day of the interment [Catherine of Aragon's funeral] the Concubine had an abortion which seemed to be a male child which she had not borne 3½ months, at which the King has shown great distress. The said Concubine wished to lay the blame on the duke of Norfolk, whom she hates, saying he frightened her by bringing the news of the fall the King had six days before. But it is well known that is not the cause, for it was told her in a way that she should not be alarmed or attach much importance to it. Some think it was owing to her own incapacity to bear children, others to a fear that the King would treat her like the late Queen, especially considering the treatment shown to a lady of the Court, named Mistress Semel, to whom, as many say, he has lately made great presents.[16]

Along with the great presents, a story has survived of Anne catching Jane sitting in her husband's lap around this time; upon seeing Anne's distress, Henry dismissed Jane and tried to placate his wife but it would later become apparent that the damage had been done. This sounds out of character for what we know of Jane and her behaviour but that's not to say it didn't happen. She could have been swept up in the moment or taken unawares or she could have felt she was doing nothing wrong. This story is not from a contemporary source, but from the account of Jane Dormer, Duchess of Feria, who may have again heard it from her mistress, Mary I.[17]

Whatever exactly caused the miscarriage, Henry was not as forgiving as he had been in the past. He stormed into a distraught Anne's bedchamber complaining about the loss of his son. Anne gave as good as she got, stating it was his fault as he had been unkind to her and that she was distressed about his relationship with 'that wench Jane Seymour'. In her distress she broke down and told him, 'Because the love I bear you is much greater than Katharine's, my heart broke, when I saw you loved others.' Henry never could take the blame for his actions and coldly responded that she 'should have no more boys by him' and that "I will speak with you when you are well' before storming out again.[18]

Some historians regard this as the beginning of the end for Anne and perhaps it was. Chapuys himself stated, 'she has miscarried of her saviour.'[19] It was certainly a significant blow to their marriage but Anne would reign for another four months before her arrest on 2 May. What was going on? Catherine was gone so he wouldn't be forced to return to her. Was Henry undecided on the future of his second marriage? Was he worried about the embarrassment caused by discarding another wife? Did he still have feelings for Anne? After her arrest her downfall was swift and brutal, taking only seventeen days. Why did these seventeen days not take place in February? Was Henry waiting for something? Anne showed incredible bravery after her final miscarriage, a heart-breaking event that hurts women as much now as it did then, telling her ladies, 'I shall be the sooner with child again, and the son I bear will not be doubtful like this one, which was conceived during the life of the Princess Dowager.'[20] It was not to be.

Anne's miscarriage would be one of the factors that would change everything for Jane. In early 1536 she had been gaining recognition as a favourite of the king, a possible mistress. But was she a future queen? She was presented as an alternative by herself and her supporters but nothing was as yet set in stone; we are without records of private conversations, between her, Henry, her family and the imperial party, but notable figures started forming around Jane in February 1536. From these allies she received coaching and advice on how to behave around the king and what to say, leading some to think she was merely a parrot repeating everything she was told; whilst she certainly took advice, she had her own beliefs, principles and goals she was working towards.

It is worth taking into account the facts as of February 1536: Anne had miscarried once, possibly twice, Henry was now aged 45 and still without a male heir, there was no universally accepted line of succession in England and Europe, and the Pope and England were no closer to accepting Anne as queen even though Catherine was gone.

Emperor Charles V by Jakob Seisenegger, c. 1532.

It would have served Jane and her family well for her to be in the king's thoughts and not forgotten. Anne had proved it was possible for an English woman to become the Queen of England so if she had done it, why couldn't Jane?

On the day of Catherine's funeral Chapuys wrote to Charles V, stating that he had been

> informed by one of the principal persons at Court that this King had said to someone in great confidence, and as it were in confession, that he had made this marriage, seduced by witchcraft, and for this reason he considered it null; and that this was evident because God did not permit them to have any male issue, and that he believed that he might take another wife, which he gave to understand that he had some wish to do. The thing is very difficult for me to believe,

although it comes from a good source. I will watch to see if there are any indications of its probability.[21]

This is the first mention of Henry discussing witchcraft in relation to Anne Boleyn, but contrary to popular belief she was never actually charged with it. Taking the date into account, if Henry had said this, it was most likely a combination of grief and anger speaking and him needing to vent; however, it was an ominous sign of how drastically 'our most dear and most entirely beloved wife the Queen' had fallen in Henry's eyes. This is also the first direct mention of him contemplating taking another wife.

There is little surviving mention of Jane during February but this almost seems in character; at this time she will have been busy discussing plans for the future or learning all she could about the king and receiving advice from her new allies. It's possible she encouraged and recruited her own supporters; she would soon have an opportunity to put what she had learnt into action.

In March Anne and her household were at Greenwich Palace but the king was elsewhere thinking about his new love; he wrote Jane a letter and sent her a purse of sovereigns. A purse of sovereigns was an unacceptable gift to a young unmarried woman and implied it was for services rendered

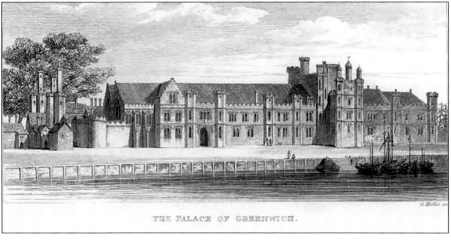

THE PALACE OF GREENWICH.

A sketch of Greenwich Palace published in the *Gentleman's Magazine* in 1840, based on earlier sources as the palace was then long since demolished. Originally published by W. Bristow, 1797, Canterbury. Jane was at Greenwich when she received a letter from the king and a purse of sovereigns; she returned both unopened aware of what the letter might contain.

or services soon to be; gifts of jewellery were acceptable though not always appropriate, but when the gift giver was the king, it was widely considered an honour no matter the eventual outcome. Jane never opened the letter but it probably included a request for her to become the king's mistress. Jane was well aware of all this and took the opportunity to tell Henry exactly where she stood. What happened was relayed to Chapuys by the Marchioness of Dorset:

> and that the young lady, after kissing the letter, returned it unopened to the messenger, and throwing herself on her knees before him, begged the said messenger that he would pray the King on her part to consider that she was a gentlewoman of good and honourable parents, without reproach, and that she had no greater riches in the world than her honour, which she would not injure for a thousand deaths, and that if he wished to make her some present in money she begged it might be when God enabled her to make some honourable match.[22]

Jane skilfully denied the king without hurting his feelings and in fact increased his respect for her. On a personal level she was likely feeling a lot of mixed emotions. She was probably a little offended and hurt by the gift of money as she was not sharing his bed at this time. She knew what it would imply if others heard of it, which they would and did; gifts were one thing, money quite another and Henry should have been aware of this. At the same time, it was a sign that Henry hadn't forgotten her and was still interested – a good sign if less than tactful.

Template of Anne Stanhope by an unknown artist, c. pre-1587. Whilst Anne has been described as a 'difficult woman', Jane got on quite well with her and the two were close.

Chapuys goes on to write of Henry's response:

by this the King's love and desire towards the said lady was wonderfully increased, and that he had said she had behaved most virtuously, and to show her that he only loved her honourably, he did not intend henceforth to speak with her except in presence of some of her kin;[23] for which reason the King has caused Cromwell to remove from a chamber to which the King can go by certain galleries without being perceived, and has lodged there the eldest brother of the said lady with his wife [Edward Seymour and Anne Stanhope], in order to bring thither the same young lady,[24] who has been well taught for the most part by those intimate with the King, who hate the concubine, that she must by no means comply with the King's wishes except by way of marriage; in which she is quite firm.

She is also advised to tell the King boldly how his marriage is detested by the people, and none consider it lawful; and on the occasion when she shall bring forward the subject, there ought to be present none but titled persons, who will say the same if the King put them upon their oath of fealty.

Whether Jane told Henry his marriage was detested by his people is unknown; but she would later prove she had the nerve to disagree with him so perhaps she later gained confidence from this and other incidents during her courtship when she stated uncomfortable facts and he didn't lash out.

Chapuys finished his report, stating:

And the said Marchioness would like that I or someone else, on the part of your Majesty, should assist in the matter; and certainly, it appears to me that if it succeeds, it will be a great thing both for the security of the Princess [Mary] and to remedy the heresies here, of which the Concubine [Anne] is the cause and principal nurse, and also to pluck the King from such an abominable and more than incestuous marriage. The Princess would be very happy, even if she were excluded from her inheritance by male issue. I will consult with them again today, and on learning her opinion will consider the expedient to be taken, so that if no good be done, I may at least not do any harm.[25]

Mary would give her full support to Anne's rival and go onto become one of Jane's closest friends.

As Jane suspected rumours of her relationship with Henry spread beyond the court into the populace, but there was not the outcry against the couple that accompanied the beginning of Henry and Anne's relationship. Jane would have probably wanted things to remain discreet for as long as possible though she cannot have been surprised that they didn't. She would have been learning to deal with the loss of her familiar anonymity and privacy at the same time as becoming the centre of attention, not ideal circumstances but she coped – she would have little choice but to do so if she became queen.

Henry himself was aware of the rumours and in the only surviving letter we have written by him to Jane, he sought to reassure her:

> My dear friend and mistress,
> The bearer of these few lines from thy entirely devoted servant will deliver into thy fair hands a token of my true affection for thee, hoping you will keep it for ever in your sincere love for me. Advertising you that there is a ballad made lately of great derision against us, which if it go much abroad and is seen by you, I pray you to pay no manner of regard to it. I am not at present informed who is the setter forth of this malignant writing, but if he is found out he shall be straitly punished for it. For the things ye lacked I have minded my lord to supply them to you as soon as he can buy them. Thus hoping shortly to receive you in these arms, I end for the present your own loving servant and sovereign,
> H. R.[26]

There is no surviving text of the ballad in question, but the words 'malignant' and 'derision' do force us to conclude that the ballad defamed the couple. Anne still had her supporters, dwindling as they may have been, and it is certainly possible one of them had spread or produced the ballad in Anne's defence. There is an alternative way of looking at the balladaa and letter: Henry himself was a notoriously private man and did not like his affairs to become known, let alone discussed or made into a ballad. 'Malignant writing' can be read and understood to be referring to gossip; 'derision' is harder to redefine in this context but it could be gossip again or Henry being dismissive of, perhaps even referring sarcastically to, the ballad. He certainly wanted Jane to pay no attention to it. This theory is possible but without the ballad itself we will never know and for now we will have to interpret the letter at face value.

In March, Edward Seymour was appointed a Gentleman of the Privy Chamber. Henry often promoted the relatives of the woman he was courting but an even greater and more public indication of his feelings was on its way. Jane had so far gained the backing of Mary, the Imperial

Sir Nicholas Carew by Hans Holbein the Younger, c. 1532/3. Originally a supporter of Anne Boleyn, he became dissatisfied with her treatment of his friends and the king and became a supporter of Catherine of Aragon and her daughter. He later supported Jane when Henry's eye fell on her. He was admitted to the Order of the Garter in April 1536 in what is believed to have been a calculated snub to Anne Boleyn's brother, George. Carew was executed after Jane's death in 1538 for his alleged involvement in the Exeter conspiracy.

Ambassador and with him the pro-Catherine faction and her old friend Sir Francis Bryan who may have been responsible for bringing one of his relatives over to her cause.

Sir Nicholas Carew had married Sir Francis's only sister Elizabeth and, like Sir Francis, was a distant relative of Anne Boleyn whom he had once supported, but he later became unhappy with her treatment of the king and his friends and began supporting Catherine and Mary. On St George's Day, 23 April 1536, Henry invested Sir Nicholas with the Order of the Garter, the most prestigious order of chivalry in England. Founded in 1348 by Edward III, the order is dedicated to England's patron saint St George and still exists today. To be invested was a great honour as it was solely at the monarch's discretion and was limited to twenty-six members at any one time, including the monarch and the Prince of Wales. So, when a vacancy became available, through death or disgrace, there was eager interest as to who would receive the coveted honour. Anne had wanted the vacancy to go to her brother but Henry chose Sir Nicholas, claiming he had promised King Francis that he would be appointed the next time there was a vacancy. It's hard to imagine Henry fulfilling an old promise to a man who was only sometimes his ally but more often his rival and enemy, Henry likely used this excuse to deflect Anne from the fact that Sir Nicholas was one of Jane's supporters; she wasn't fooled. There survives an account of the day's events:

> On St George's Day, 23 April, a chapter of the Order of the Garter was held at Greenwich, at which were present the King, the dukes of Richmond and Norfolk, the earls of Northumberland, Westmoreland, Wiltshire, Sussex, Rutland, and Oxford, lord Sandys, and Sir Wm. Fitzwilliam. It was determined to hold the feast on May 21, the earl of Northumberland taking the Sovereign's place, assisted by the earls of Rutland, Westmoreland, and Oxford, and Sir Wm. Fitzwilliam. Votes were taken for the election of a knight; and the next day, after mass for the dead, the King declared Sir Nic. Carew elected. He was installed when the feast was kept, on May 21.[27]

Chapuys who was also aware of the relevance of this appointment informed the emperor:

The Grand Ecuyer, Mr. Caro, had on St George's day the Order of the Garter in the place of the deceased M. de Burgain (lord Abergavenny), to the great disappointment of Rochford, who was seeking for it, and all the more because the Concubine has not had sufficient influence to get it for her brother; and it will not be the fault of the said Ecuyer if the Concubine, although his cousin be not dismounted. He continually counsels Mrs. Semel and other conspirators and only four days ago he and some persons of the chamber sent to tell the Princess to be of good cheer, for shortly the opposite party would put water in their

Thomas Cromwell by Hans Holbein the Younger, c. 1532/3. Henry VIII's right-hand man, he allied with Jane and her supporters when he believed Anne was becoming a threat to him; his only son Gregory married Jane's sister Elizabeth in August 1537, thereby creating a familial link.

wine, for the King was already as sick and tired of the concubine as could be; and the brother of lord Montague told me yesterday at dinner that the day before the bishop of London had been asked if the King could abandon the said concubine, and he would not give any opinion to anyone but the King himself, and before doing so he would like to know the King's own inclination, meaning to intimate that the King might leave the said concubine, but that, knowing his fickleness, he would not put himself in danger.[28]

It was a very public snub and there was very little Anne could do about it; however, she did strike back in another direction, inadvertently providing Jane with her final powerful ally.

Anne had instructed her almoner John Skip to preach before the court against a new policy of Cromwell's which involved closing the smaller monasteries and redirecting the funds into the royal coffers. Anne believed the funds should be redistributed to more charitable and educational purposes. Skip chose as his sermon the story of Haman and Ahasuerus from the Old Testament: Ahasuerus had been persuaded by his chief minister Haman to order the massacre of the Jews but Ahasuerus's good wife Esther counselled him against the plan and instead Haman himself was hanged. It is not difficult to see who was who in this allegory and Cromwell took the sign for what it was, a warning. The two had once been close allies but had come to have increasingly opposing views and were on bad terms with each other, with Anne once claiming she would have his head – a fact that is corroborated by Chapuys who had discussed the possibility of another marriage with Cromwell:

> I told Cromwell that I had for some time forborne to visit him that he might not incur suspicion of his mistress for the talk he had previously held with me, well remembering that he had previously told me she would like to see his head cut off. This I could not forget for the love I bore him; and I could not but wish him a more gracious mistress, and one more grateful for the inestimable services he had done the King, and that he must beware of enraging her, else he must never expect perfect reconciliation; in which case I hoped he would see to it better than did the Cardinal, as I had great belief in his dexterity and prudence; and if it was true, what I had heard, that the King was treating for a new marriage, it would be the way to avoid much evil, and be very much for the advantage of his master, who had been hitherto disappointed of male issue, and who knows quite well, whatever they may say or preach, that this marriage will never be held as lawful, for several reasons which he might sufficiently understand.[29]

Cromwell had once been employed by Cardinal Wolsey and he had witnessed the end of the man who had failed Henry and Anne, and he had no intention of following the same path. Following the sermon, which displeased her husband as well, Cromwell joined the Seymour faction and worked to bring about the downfall of another queen of England and the rise of a third in her place.

The one person missing from this collaboration is Henry; he still had not committed to any course of action and in fact was still trying to gain recognition of his second queen whilst others were planning to bring the marriage to an end. On 18 April 1536 it has been suggested that Eustace Chapuys was finally tricked into acknowledging Anne by bowing to her. Until recently I had thought the same but Sylvia Barbara Soberton, author of the *Forgotten Tudor Women* books, raised the interesting point that he never actually spoke to her, had an audience or kissed her cheek, which would be more sure signs of recognition. A bow could be simply read as common courtesy, the equivalent of which would be a gentleman tipping or removing his hat when coming across a lady in more modern times.

If you read Chapuys' account of the event itself, it doesn't sound as if he attached too much importance to it, even allowing for him trying to talk himself out of trouble with the emperor; there is no outrage or horror at being tricked or disgust at finally coming face to face with the woman who had wrecked Queen Catherine and her daughter's lives and torn England from Rome. When he arrived at court on 18 April, Cromwell had asked him if he wished to visit and kiss the queen as this would greatly please the king but that it was entirely his choice. Chapuys refused. Chapuys then explained what happened next:

> I was conducted to mass by lord Rochford, the concubine's brother, and when the King came to the offering there was a great concourse of people partly to see how the concubine and I behaved to each other. She was courteous enough, for when I was behind the door by which she entered, she returned, merely to do me reverence as I did to her. After mass the King went to dine at the concubine's lodging, whither everybody accompanied him except myself, who was conducted by Rochford to the King's Chamber of Presence, and dined there with all the principal men of the Court. I am told the concubine asked the King why I did not enter there as the other ambassadors did, and the King replied that it was not without good reason.[30]

The sentence 'concourse of people partly to see how the concubine and I behaved to each other' implies he knew he would at least see Anne that day, that he wasn't tricked into it. When word reached Mary of what had happened, she was understandably upset as to what this implied, as Chapuys writes in another letter to a correspondent a few days later:

Although I would not kiss or speak to the Concubine, the Princess and other good persons have been somewhat jealous at the mutual reverences required by politeness which were done at the church. I refused to visit her until I had spoken to the King. If I had seen any hope from the King's answer, I would have offered not two but 100 candles to the shedevil, although another thing made me unwilling, viz., that I was told she was not in favour with the King; besides, Cromwell was quite of my opinion that I should do well to wait till I had spoken to the King. Even before receiving instructions from the Emperor, has always avoided 'l'envoy' which the Princess urged, as again she has since done, for the reasons which he has heretofore written.[31]

Chapuys still referred to her as the 'concubine' and 'shedevil' and the phrase 'required by politeness' doesn't sound like acknowledgement to me but perhaps it was enough for Henry. It has been suggested that he couldn't let go of his second marriage unless someone 'outside England' had acknowledged it; if he ended his marriage to Anne without it, it would look like Henry was inadvertently admitting everyone else had been right all along, something Henry could never face. Was this the moment Henry decided that their marriage was over? It was well known that he no longer loved Anne, that he was tired of her. She hadn't given him a son and she wasn't accepted in England or outside as his wife and queen. If he was still wavering Cromwell was about to give him a nudge.

Cromwell had begun receiving reports about behaviour in the Queen's Household. It's difficult to tell if he started digging for them or gossip was brought to his attention that he took further; either way the end, tragic result was the same. He interviewed her ladies and servants and learned there was a degree of inappropriate flirtatiousness and closeness between Anne and a few male courtiers; he also discovered that Anne had clashed with Henry Norris following a conversation over why he had not proposed to her cousin as yet. The conversation strayed into dangerous territory when Anne told him, 'you look for dead men's shoes, for if ought come to the king but good you would look to have me.'[32] This was imagining the king's death and this was treason. Anne had quickly realised her mistake and made Norris go to her almoner and swear that she was a good woman but news of this conversation was all over the court within hours.

On 30 April Cromwell invited Anne's musician Mark Smeaton to dine with him, but shortly after he arrived, he was arrested and quickly confessed to adultery with the queen; this was almost certainly extracted through torture as he was not of noble blood and he had no protection against this recourse. Almost like a domino effect, events moved swiftly after this. The next day the king and queen attended the May Day jousts at Greenwich and at first all appeared well but, after receiving a message, Henry suddenly stood and left without saying a word, taking Henry Norris with him. This was the last time Anne saw her husband.

As they rode away Henry questioned Norris about his relationship with the queen, offering him a pardon if he confessed the truth: either Henry had heard of Anne and Norris's confrontation days earlier or Cromwell had informed him of the results of the investigations he was undertaking. Whatever made Henry suspicious of Norris, he steadfastly defended himself and the queen against any wrongdoing. He was arrested the next day and joined Smeaton in the Tower of London. On the same day, George Boleyn was arrested and soon after, his sister, the queen herself,

The Tower of London. Once a royal palace, during Henry VIII's reign it quickly became a prison and gained its frightening reputation. Anne Boleyn and Catherine Howard were beheaded inside its walls; Jane was rowed past days after Anne execution as part of the celebrations for her own marriage – what she thought of the horrific events that had taken place days earlier we don't know. (*Author's Collection*)

was taken to the Tower on charges of adultery. Four more arrests would be made: on 4 May Sirs William Brereton and Francis Weston and on 8 May Sirs Thomas Wyatt and Richard Page joined them; the latter two would be the only ones to leave alive.

Anne's and the gentlemen's arrest were nothing short of a setup but Cromwell had planned well and used believable suspects. All these men were known to be close to the queen, they had received patronage and favour from her but the most any of them had done was flirt in the 'courtly fashion' and whilst this could be inadvisable it wasn't worth the price they paid. The most shocking accusation against Anne was the charge of incest with her own brother, an accusation that was little believed then as now but was likely used as part of the mudslinging campaign to destroy her and her reputation and to show how evil she was and how right Henry was to take action against her.

What did Henry think? Outsiders came to the conclusion that he believed the charges against her and even added to them, claiming that his son and elder daughter were lucky to escape with their lives as Anne had planned to poison them and that he believed she had slept with over a hundred men. Henry was very skilled at convincing himself he was never in the wrong and that each of his actions was justified, but to ruin a woman he had once been passionately in love with shows a new degree of coldness hitherto unseen and Jane would have been wise to take heed of this.

The trials themselves were a farce; as Norris, Brereton, Smeaton and Weston were found guilty the day before Anne's own trial, it was hardly likely she would be found innocent of adultery when they had been found guilty of it. It has now been proved that some of the dates when she was supposedly sleeping with the men were easily contradicted by court records; either Anne or the men were in different places on the date in question or Anne was recovering from childbirth, a time when no woman wants relations with a man. Anne and George were tried separately from the others due to their high status. They both disputed the accusations against them and answered the questions thrown at them calmly and wisely, so much so that there were bets laid that George might be found innocent, but he read out a statement that he had been expressly told not to regarding the king's ability to father children and some witnesses believed that condemned him. Perhaps it did, or perhaps George knew there was no way out and decided to take a parting shot at the king before he fell as revenge for the destruction of his sister, his friends and himself. Both Anne and George were found guilty. George was sentenced to beheading whilst Anne was sentenced to be burned or beheaded at the king's pleasure.

In what was believed to be a final act of mercy for the woman he had once loved so much, Henry decided she would be beheaded, not with an axe, but by a French swordsman; however, this is actually the final proof that Henry and Cromwell were never going to allow Anne to live. In order for the swordsman to have been there to execute Anne on the original date, 18 May, he had to have been summoned in advance. Claire Ridgeway of the *Anne Boleyn Files* has worked out that, allowing for travelling time, the latest he must have been summoned was 12 or 13 May and the earliest the 9th or 10th. Anne Boleyn's trial was held on 15 May.

On 19 May 1536 Queen Anne Boleyn walked the short distance from her apartments to the scaffold on Tower Green, where she made a short speech to the crowd:

Good Christian people, I have not come here to preach a sermon; I have come here to die. For according to the law and by the law I am judged to die, and therefore I will speak nothing against it. I am come hither to accuse no man, nor to speak of that whereof I am accused and condemned to die, but I pray God save the King and send him long to reign over you, for a gentler nor a more merciful prince was there never, and to me he was ever a good, a gentle, and sovereign lord. And if any person will meddle of my cause, I require them to judge the best. And thus I take my leave of the world and of you all, and I heartily desire you all to pray for me … O Lord have mercy on me, to God I commend my soul. To Jesus Christ I commend my soul; Lord Jesu receive my soul.[33]

There are different versions of Anne's final speech; some are similar to each other but one of them is markedly different from the others and is taken from the *Spanish Chronicle*. *The Spanish Chronicle*, or *The Chronicle of King Henry VIII of England* is an account written by an unknown author that recorded events from Henry's and Edward VI's reigns. Filled with enough salacious and inaccurate detail to make it a 'gossip column', it is regarded today by many historians as inaccurate but contains the following version of Anne's speech:

> Do not think, good people, that I am sorry to die, or that I have done anything to deserve this death. My fault has been my great pride, and the great crime I committed in getting the King to leave my mistress Queen Katherine for my sake, and I pray God to pardon me for it. I say to you all that everything they have accused me of is false, and the principal reason I am to die is Jane Seymour, as I was the cause of the ill that befell my mistress.[34]

Given that the same account mixes up the order of the marriages of Anne of Cleves and Catherine Howard and records that Lord Rochford was Catherine Parr's brother, I think we can dismiss this version. Anne may have thought it but she never said it. She was leaving behind an infant daughter and surviving family members. She could not afford to take the risk that Henry would take his anger out on them.

Anne Boleyn was beheaded with one clean stroke.

Who brought down Anne? Cromwell? Henry? Jane? All three can be held responsible for the end of the marriage but Jane today usually receives much vitriol from Anne supporters for her part in Anne's death, but did she have one? I don't think so.

Looking at the surviving evidence, all the sources talk of 'bringing the marriage to an end', 'setting Anne aside' and Jane replacing Anne as queen: from Jane, the Seymours and the imperial party there is no mention of killing or destroying anyone, not that this would have been directly written down but there are no allusions to it either. Jane may have felt little guilt in replacing Anne in Henry's affections; she had seen Anne do the same to Catherine after all and as she was a devout Catholic, she may have believed (like many others) that Anne's marriage was invalid anyway. Jane did absolutely nothing that Anne herself hadn't done years earlier.

But did Anne Boleyn have to die? We can agree that Henry wouldn't have wanted the problems associated with another ex-wife hanging around, especially as he had just been freed by the death of the first one. He was intimately aware of the risks and problems another discarded wife would cause; however, Europe and England as a whole did not regard

Anne's marriage as valid so in one way it would have been easier to set her aside and very little comment would have been made. But Anne was a smart woman; she was a politician and a strategist with a child to fight for. Like Catherine before her, she would not have stood quietly aside and let her daughter be disinherited. In a cruel, sick way Anne's destruction was a back-handed compliment to her intelligence and ability; she was simply too dangerous to be left alive. In the end there are only two people responsible for Anne's death: her husband Henry and Thomas Cromwell.

Chapter 7

The Third Quene

Jane did not witness the arrests or legal proceedings against Anne and the men tried with her; she had retired from the court days before. Henry wanted Jane kept out of events as much as possible so she retired to Sir Nicholas Carew's residence in Surrey. Whether Henry asked Carew to look after Jane or Carew volunteered is unknown but as the two were recent allies and perhaps even friends it made sense for Jane to stay with him.

It must have been disconcerting to be removed from court just as her star was rising and perhaps, she worried it meant Henry was tiring of her but when she later heard of the events that had taken place, she was probably glad to be out of it. She was not cut off and news would have reached her from her brother, Carew and perhaps Henry himself of Anne's supposed crimes and how the trial was progressing. She knew she would be the Queen of England very soon and had already had a taste of what was to come. Whilst staying with Carew she was given the best rooms in the house and her every whim was catered for.

Did she believe Anne was guilty as charged? We don't know but it must have occurred to her at some point how well timed these accusations were. Did she question the charges? Anne was well known to be flirtatious and had a poor reputation where her morals were concerned; she had 'stolen' Henry from Catherine and it would not be outside the realm of

Signature of Queen Jane Seymour.

Surviving tapestries at Hampton Court Palace today. Extremely valuable at the time and considered priceless today, they would have been vibrantly coloured in Jane's lifetime. (*Author's collection*)

possibility that she had gone too far with another man. At this time Jane was more focused on the excitement of becoming queen and how quickly this had come about; Anne had waited years, Jane months. How did she feel when she realised Anne was to be executed and not sent away? If she genuinely believed her guilty as charged then perhaps nothing, but if she had her suspicions, even later, she may have told herself that this was Anne's punishment for her behaviour towards the former queen and princess.

One message she received from Henry will have given her pause for thought as he told her she would receive news of Anne's condemnation by 3 pm on 15 May.[1] Jane now definitely knew Anne was going to be found guilty even before her trial which must have made her uncomfortable; there wasn't even the pretence of an inquiry on Henry's part.

Aside from telling his new love that the trial was clearly a formality, it revealed another side to Henry that Jane may not have seen before up close. Henry had once loved Anne; he had changed England to obtain her, but after her failure to provide a son, a vengeful Henry had turned on her and destroyed her completely. This was the same man who was now in love with her and whom she may have been in love with or at the very least had feelings for and thought fondly of. Jane now knew first-hand how dangerous the king could be and what would happen if she 'let him down' or if he turned on her.

After a few days apart Jane was brought to a large mansion in Chelsea about a mile from the court and Henry; he had missed her and wanted to spend time with her. At Chelsea she was 'splendidly served by the king's cook and other officers' and received a magnificent new wardrobe which she was careful to prepare and maintain for her first public appearance as queen.[2] During their time together Henry and Jane spoke of their plans for the future and Jane took the opportunity to speak for Mary, an action that was reported to Chapuys who wrote she

> proposed to him to replace the Princess to her former position; and on the king telling her that she must be out of her senses to think of such a thing, and that she ought to study the welfare and exaltation of her own children, if she had any by him, instead of looking out for the good of others, the said Jane Seymour replied that in soliciting the Princess's reinstatement she thought she was asking for the good, the repose, and tranquillity of himself, of the children they might themselves have, and of the kingdom in general, inasmuch as should the reinstatement not take place, neither Your Majesty nor the English people would be satisfied, and the ruin and desolation of the country would inevitably ensue.[3]

It has been claimed that words were often put into Jane's mouth, but it was well known, then and now, the high regard and affection she held for Mary. Is it too much to believe she came up with this response herself? It would certainly match with the traits and beliefs that have been ascribed to Jane: loyalty, kindness, sensibility, amiability?

With unseemly haste Jane was betrothed to Henry the day after Anne's execution. The betrothal was kept very discreet for obvious reasons but news of it soon leaked out. Whilst Anne had never been popular, there was much muttering about the way Henry had behaved and reacted following the revelations; the timing of their betrothal left much to be desired in the eyes of the people, though there was never the outright condemnation and anger as there had been with Henry and Anne's marriage.[4]

From Henry's perspective, he may not have understood the benefits of waiting a short time. Anne and her lovers had been found guilty; therefore, he was doing nothing wrong, time was passing, he wasn't getting any younger and he still had no son and heir. If we look at this from only a logical perspective it all makes sense but Henry was rarely ruled by logic; in fact he was often ruled by his own will, which he believed was the will of God. What he wanted he got as it was God's will and right then he wanted Jane and a son. However, a letter from Cromwell to Stephen Gardiner, Bishop of Winchester, dated 5 July 1536 contains an interesting excerpt that reveals how Henry 'put a spin' on events: 'Doubts not he knows that the king is married again. He has chosen, as all his nobles and council upon their knees moved him to do, the most virtuous lady and veriest gentlewoman that liveth.'[5]

We know that Henry did what Henry wanted and by this time so did his counsellors. They would rarely contradict him or do anything without his express command especially when it came to matters of his heart and the succession; they were also very well aware of the existence of Jane. They could have begged him to remarry – it is not outside the realm of possibility – however, would they dare? Elizabeth Norton believes Henry did instruct his council to ask him to marry again to which he, as a good

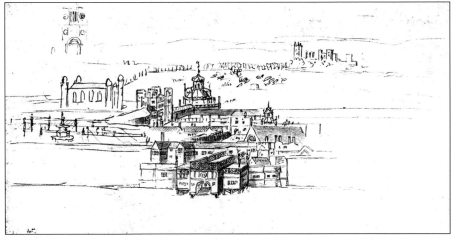

The Palace of Whitehall by Antony van den Wyngaerde, c. 1554–7. Jane and Henry were married in the Queen's Closet at the palace.

Catherine Parr married Henry VIII as his sixth and final wife in the Privy Closet at Hampton Court Palace. Today this room is set up to show visitors how the room may have looked. This gives us an idea of how the Queen's Closet at the Palace of Whitehall was set up for Jane's marriage to Henry in 1536. (*Author's Collection*)

king and master, would graciously agree for the good of the country. *The Chronicle of Henry VIII* has the king telling his council: 'I bear much good will to Jane Seymour, and I beg you will approve of her for my wife.' To which the council eagerly responded: 'Let your majesty do as you desire. We all consider her a worthy maiden, and we hope in God that your union will be fruitful and happy.'[6]

After their betrothal Jane's whereabouts again become unclear with some believing she returned to her family home; in fact, a later legend claimed that the couple were married at Wolf Hall and held their celebrations there; however, it is more likely given the time between her betrothal and her marriage that she returned to the property at Chelsea, a property that allowed her to be close to her future husband.

Jane was married to Henry on 30 May 1536 in the Queen's Closet at Whitehall Palace,[7] eleven days after her predecessor's execution. Three days later she made her first public appearance as queen at Greenwich

Palace. An excerpt from a letter written by Sir John Russell to Henry's uncle, Lord Lisle, describes the occasion:

> On Friday last [2 June] the Queen sat abroad as Queen, and was served by her own servants, who were sworn that same day. The King came in his great boat to Greenwich that day with his privy chamber, and the Queen and the ladies in the great barge. I assure you she is as gentle a lady as ever I knew, and as fair a Queen as any in Christendom. The King hath come out of hell into heaven for the gentleness in this and the cursedness and the unhappiness in the other. You would do well to write to the King again that you rejoice he is so well matched with so gracious a woman as is reported. This will please the King.[8]

On Whitsunday two days later, Jane was formally proclaimed Queen of England. Splendidly dressed as befitted her new station, she walked in procession to Mass attended by a great number of her ladies and was prayed for as queen for the first time, which would have been a humbling experience. Afterwards she swore in her household and was later seen dining in her presence chamber under the cloth of estate. That same day she experienced her first diplomatic encounter as queen when she received a visit from the Imperial Ambassador. Chapuys recorded the exchange:

> Mass over, I accompanied the King to the apartments of the queen, whom, with the king's pleasure, I kissed, congratulating her on her marriage and wishing her prosperity. I told her besides that although the device of the lady who had preceded her on the throne was 'the happiest of women', I had no doubt she herself would fully realise that motto. I was (said I) sure that your majesty would be equally rejoiced with such a virtuous and amiable queen, the more so that her brother had once been in your majesty's service.

He also took the opportunity to remind her of Mary's difficult situation and begged her to continue to show favour to her, telling Jane: 'without having had the pain and trouble of bringing her into the world, had such a daughter that she would receive more pleasure and consolation from her than any other she might have.'[9]

The arms of Henry VIII and Queen Jane Seymour held aloft by angels outside the Chapel Royal at Hampton Court Palace. (Author's Collection)

This was incredibly presumptuous and insensitive on the ambassador's part but Jane tactfully promised to do all she could and in return Chapuys complimented her by suggesting that she would earn the name 'Pacificator' for her efforts.

It is possible that Jane was starting to struggle at this point as Henry interceded, explaining that this was her first official encounter with an ambassador as queen and made excuses for her. Whilst we can be fairly certain she understood French, she may not have been completely fluent in the language that Chapuys was conversing in; however; it is equally possible that Henry did not want her to be influenced by the ambassador or even become too involved in political affairs.

On 7 June a magnificent water pageant was held in her honour. The king and queen were escorted downriver by the lords and ladies of the court dressed in their best clothes and jewellery; she also received gun salutes in her honour. Perhaps a display from Chapuys added to the special occasion as recorded in *Wriothesley's Chronicle:* 'at Radcliffe the Emperoures Embassadour stoode in a tente with a banner of the Emperoures armes set in the top of his tente and divers banners about

Jane Seymour from the workshop of Hans Holbein the Younger, c. 1540.

Self portrait of Hans Holbein the Younger, c. 1542/3. It is thanks to Holbein's excellent work that we have such a good idea what Jane looked like.

the same, he himself being in a rych gowne of purple satten, with divers gentlemen standing about him with gownes and cottes of velvett.'[10]

Chapuys had arranged for two boats of musicians to row out and serenade the new queen and he even provided his own gun salute. As a staunch supporter of Catherine and Mary, he had barely had any interaction with Anne and he certainly would never have greeted her this way. There was surely a touch of quid pro quo and ingratiation in this display as with their discussion days earlier but it's worth remembering he didn't have to do this or go this far; he could have achieved his objectives through future personal contact with Jane. They had been officially introduced, he had supported her prior to her queenship and they both had similar beliefs and interests.

Despite their common goals though, he had at one point not believed the relationship would last or understand what Henry saw in her; he had held these opinions just weeks before her marriage to the king, writing to one correspondent: 'She is sister of one Edward Semel, of middle stature and no great beauty, so fair that one would call her rather pale than otherwise. She is over 25 years old.'

In the same letter he went onto speculate whether she was a virgin as she had been so long at court but decided that if Henry tired of her, he could easily find witnesses to say she wasn't. He described her as not having great wit but perhaps good understanding, and that she was inclined to be proud and haughty.[11]

To modern eyes the letter seems harsh especially coming from a supporter and the comments about her virginity are unfair. No scandals were ever attached to Jane's name and she walked away from her failed earlier betrothal with her reputation intact. There is no arguing the fact that Jane had not received the same high standard of education that her predecessors had but Catherine and Anne were the exceptions rather than the rule. Jane received a thoroughly normal education for the time to prepare her for her role as wife, mother and mistress of her husband's estate and she would soon prove that she had good tact and understanding on many occasions. As for her haughtiness, Chapuys is the only surviving account we have of it; other surviving sources describe her as amiable, kind and gentle. Even Cromwell, a man not immediately known for giving compliments and praise, wrote: 'Soo hath his grace I thinke chose the vertuost lady and the veriest gentlewoman that lyveth and oon that variethe asmoche from the conditions of thother [Anne] as the daye varietie from the night.'[12]

He may have been laying it on a bit thick in trying to distance the new queen from the old but it's a rare insight into his thoughts; he is recorded as saying that nature had wronged Catherine of Aragon by not making her a man because if she had been she would have surpassed all the heroes in history. I'm not however saying Jane may not have come across as haughty. She was clearly a woman used to being in the background and overlooked, so to suddenly become the centre of attention and in such a public role would have required

Seventeenth-century miniature of Jane Seymour by painter and engraver Wencelaus Hollar. Jane's famously pale complexion manages to shine through in any image of her.

some serious adjustment that may have left her floundering for a short time, the result was to try and keep her distance and retreat into silence which may have come across as rudeness or arrogance.

Chapuys did note she bore great love and reverence for Mary but was unsure if her new position would cause her to forget her; he must have been reassured by their conversation on the 4th that she wouldn't.

Incomplete painting produced by the 'Cast Shadow Workshop', c. 1536, during Jane's first year as queen. It's possible this portrait was begun later and progress halted with Jane's sudden death; however, it is unclear why it was never finished as she continued to appear in other portraits well after her death.

Jane's first appearance as queen was a success and, despite the unseemly timing of her marriage, the court and the people of England responded well to her. She may have relied on this knowledge when Henry revealed that he had spotted two very beautiful ladies at court and that he may have rushed into his third marriage. Was this an insensitive joke by the new groom or did he mean it? He had appeared to want and love her only weeks earlier. Either way, it reminded Jane that she was not completely secure despite all the signs and celebrations.

In Tudor times (and earlier) a desirable queen was one who was pious, kind and who interceded with the king on others' behalf. She could obtain mercy for those in distress, often performed charitable obligations and, most importantly, produced children (preferably male). Jane was not yet pregnant so the first proof of her abilities as queen would be through intercession.

The unhappy Mary lurked in the background of the celebrations and was not far from her father's or Jane's thoughts. She had believed that with Anne gone, her beloved father would come to his senses, realise his mistakes and reconcile with her, that everything that had come before had been Anne's fault. Sadly, this was to prove an inaccurate take on the matter but in fairness to Mary, it was not her fault that she believed this. Until her parent's marriage fell apart, Mary had only ever seen them as a united, loving couple; she had been the apple of their eyes. She was shielded from any relationship problems by her parents and her loyal household staff and may only have become aware of her father's infidelity with the arrival of her half-brother, Henry Fitzroy, in 1519 or soon after.

When it became clear Anne Boleyn was not going to be just another mistress and that she was going to have to fight for her marriage, Catherine always maintained it was Anne's influence that took her husband from her and, if she could be removed from his side, he would return to her and be the man she still loved again, or at least this is what she maintained publicly. Catherine was not a fool and she

Lady Mary Tudor, later Mary I by Hans Holbein the Younger, c. 1536. Jane remained loyal to Mary and wanted her reinstated as heir and as part of the family. She didn't achieve the former but after her submission to her father, Mary would become one of Jane's closest friends and Jane would make every effort to include her; the two were often together and like her father, Mary was devastated by Jane's death, even falling ill soon after.

had seen her husband have affairs and turn on others before; she knew what he was capable of, she had been married to him for over twenty years so if anyone could claim to know Henry, it was Catherine. Perhaps she couldn't bring herself to face the fact the man she still loved was in love with someone else. Perfectly understandable but it did Mary a great disservice that she did not better prepare her for what her father could be like. Again, an understandable action – she did not want to ruin her daughter's vision of her beloved father, but it left Mary woefully unprepared for Henry the king; all she had ever known was Henry the father.

Henry was annoyed by the trouble Mary had caused him; as a dutiful child she owed him her obedience and loyalty, and as her king this was even more imperative. She had no right to question his actions or to stand against him and he was well aware that his people looked to her as a symbol of the old ways and that she could be used as a figurehead in rebellion against him; it was essential he neutralise her as a threat and that would involve her complete submission.

Eager to reconcile, Mary made the first move: she wrote to Cromwell asking him to help and intercede on her behalf. Cromwell replied favourably, promising to assist but warned that she would be required to submit to the king's wishes and the laws of England as they stood. Whether Mary recognised this for the warning it was or believed she could get around this uncomfortable business, she wrote to her father shortly after for the first time in years asking for his blessing and begging to be allowed to see him. Henry did not respond directly; instead, he ordered a series of articles to be drawn up and presented to her. She was to be asked outright if she recognised her father's laws, that he was the Supreme Head of the Church of England and would she acknowledge her mother's marriage had been invalid and that she was therefore illegitimate.

Mary, as everyone probably suspected, refused to acknowledge or sign the articles and the nervous commissioners had to report their failure to a furious king. A sign of how dangerous the situation was becoming, saw the Duke of Norfolk threatening physical violence:

> she was such an unnatural daughter as to disobey completely the king's injunctions, he could hardly believe that she was the king's own bastard daughter. Were she his or any other man's daughter, he would beat her to death, or strike her head against the wall until he made it as soft as a boiled apple.[13]

There was a very real chance Henry would now proceed against her as a traitor. The Privy Council was constantly in conference and known allies and friends of Mary suddenly found themselves under suspicion, expelled from court and even arrested. A traitor's punishment was execution and the fact she was his daughter would not save her; it had not saved his second wife after all. Henry was more furious than he ever had been and his patience was wearing thin; even Jane's intercession couldn't calm him. Cromwell threatened to wash his hands of the whole business and told her he regretted sticking his neck out for her and threatened to leave her to her fate if she did not comply and sign the articles. Mary was in an agonising position and along with the threat to her and her friends, she had to wage a constant battle with her head and her heart. Her conscience told her that her parents' marriage was legitimate, that she was the rightful princess of England and the Pope was the head of the Church. She wanted to obey her father but she believed his actions were wrong. Her mother had never wavered and had died standing by her beliefs; it would be a betrayal of her to give in now.

However, everything had changed since her mother's death. Mary was virtually alone, her friends were under attack, her allies were limited in what they could do for her despite how much they wanted to help (Jane included) and she herself was coming close to being tried for treason; she knew she would be found guilty as the situation stood. Henry had proved that he was capable of acting against once-cherished loved ones.

With a heavy heart and a guilty conscience, Mary gave up her and her mother's fight and signed the articles; she never even read them. She acknowledged her father as her sovereign and recognised his laws, she acknowledged him as the Supreme Head of the Church of England under Christ, and repudiated the 'pretended authority of the bishop of Rome' and, most upsetting of all, acknowledged that the marriage between the king and her mother to have 'been by God's law and man's law incestuous and unlawful'.

She then humbly wrote to her father in humiliating and excruciating tones:

Most humbly prostrate before the feet of your most excellent majesty, your most humble, faithful, and obedient subject, which hath so extremely offended your most gracious highness that mine heavy and fearful heart dares not presume to call you father, nor your majesty hath any cause by my deserts, saving the benignity of your most blessed nature doth surmount all evils, offences, and trespasses, and is ever merciful and ready to accept the penitent, calling for grace in any convenient time.[14]

She went on to acknowledge her offences and her folly in defying her father's laws and told him she would never stray from her submission and

The Clarence black bull displaying a Tudor rose (part of the king's beasts at the entrance of Hampton Court Palace). (*Author's Collection*)

would willingly obey him in all things and if he found fault with her in future, she would not presume to ask for his pity or compassion. In a later letter she informed her father that she was praying for 'the preservation of your highness, with the Queen's grace, and that it may please Him to send you issue'.[15]

Mary would never forgive herself for signing away everything she believed in and what her mother had stood for and was known to be sorrowful for a time after; she cheered slightly when Chapuys told her the

The Mortimer lion displaying Queen Jane Seymour's badge (part of the king's beasts at the entrance of Hampton Court Palace). (*Author's Collection*)

Pope would understand and even provide a dispensation for her actions as they were taken under duress.

Mary was safe, the immediate danger had passed and Henry responded to his eldest daughter with all his old warmth and affection. Mary's submission was greeted by the court with relief and happiness and Jane would have been happy to see Mary save herself even at the great personal cost it had taken. There are no known surviving letters between Jane and Mary in these trying days but that doesn't mean she didn't write to her stepdaughter. We know she had tried to intercede for her but had been rebuffed by her husband, but Jane understood tact and discretion and may have sent verbal if not written messages offering advice and support.

Mary definitely wrote to Jane shortly after and it is interesting to note that she references letters she has already received from Jane, however these could have been written post-reconciliation:

> My duty most humbly remembered to your grace, pleaseth the same to be advertised that I have received your most gracious letters, being no less full of motherly joy for my towardness of reconciliation than of most prudent council for my further proceeding therein, which your grace, of your most abundant fondness, promiseth to travail to bring to a perfection, as most benignly you have commenced and begun the matter of the same; the inestimable comfort which I have conceived of that most joyful promise like as I cannot with tongue or pen express, so, with heart and mind, this I shall assure your highness, that from this day forward neither shall mine office want to the king's majesty, my most merciful and benign father, who hath the whole disposition of mine heart in his noble hand, ne yet my service to your grace, to serve you as humbly, gladly, and obediently, with my hands under your noble feet, as is possible to be devised or imagined. Most humbly beseeching your grace, with such acceleration as should stand with your pleasure, to have in your gracious remembrance (touching the accomplishment of my most hearty desire) for the attaining of the king's most noble presence.
>
> Your Grace's most humble and obedient daughter and handmaid, Mary.[16]

Now that Mary was back in favour, Jane set about reuniting father and daughter face to face and in July, they made a short journey to meet privately with her. Whilst Henry valued his privacy in certain areas, he would have wanted a public reconciliation with his daughter to show his enemies that she could not be used against him anymore but he may have been persuaded against it. Father and daughter had not seen each other properly for a number of years and they had been publicly at odds just as long, so a private meeting was an excellent way to re-establish the relationship and if the meeting was to turn awkward and emotions ran

Jane Seymour by an unknown artist, attributed to the British (English) School, c. nineteenth century.

high, this would not be witnessed by the court. This sounds very much like something Jane would have suggested, a tactful, private smoothing over of relations.

Portrait of Henry VIII after Hans Holbein the Younger, c. 1537. Henry had a poor reputation as a husband that only worsened after Jane's death but he always claimed she was his 'true wife' and was devastated by her death.

Henry and Mary met for the first time in Jane's chambers, and the meeting appears to have gone well with Henry again the doting father of Mary's younger years and Jane embracing and kissing her stepdaughter; the trio reportedly spoke for hours in private. Henry presented his daughter with 1,000 crowns for her small pleasures and was overheard speaking about the restoration of her household whilst Jane gave her a diamond ring and showed her much affection. They were soon forced to depart to return to official business: Henry was overseeing a new Act of Succession.

The Second Act of Succession, as it became known, described Jane as the 'right noble, virtuous, and excellent lady, Queen Jane, your true and lawful wife, and have lawfully celebrated and solemnised marriage with her according to the laws of Holy Church'. Its main aim was to legitimise Henry and Jane's marriage and most importantly stated that the children of our 'most dear and entirely beloved lawful wife Queen Jane' would become the heirs to the throne of England. Mary and Elizabeth were now both equally regarded as illegitimate and unable to inherit the throne.

One part of the act that will have given Jane pause stated if she did not produce sons, then the sons of a subsequent wife would inherit the throne. In normal circumstances this may not have raised any eyebrows – it was imperative that kings set out the succession as clearly as possible and a good king planned for hypothetical events such as illness or death – but Henry had already got rid of two wives in a short space of time, on the surface for two different reasons, but underneath the same: they had not produced a son. In the summer of 1536, there was no indication that Jane was pregnant and whilst they had only been married just over a month, it would have put pressure on her.

In an unprecedented move the Act went further, stating that if Henry had no legitimate sons, he now had the power to nominate his own heir; at this time people believed the Act was referring to Henry Fitzroy, Duke of Richmond, then aged 17. If this was the intention it made logical sense; since Henry had no legitimate children, surely it would be wiser to promote the only male. If this was Henry's plan it was doomed to failure as Fitzroy died of consumption on 23 July 1536. Fitzroy's loss devasted the king on a personal and political level: he now had no son at all. He ordered that his funeral be kept as discreet as possible but was furious when he heard his son's coffin had been transported to his tomb in a straw-filled carriage in a terrible misunderstanding by the servants of the Duke of Norfolk. Jane would have comforted her husband during this difficult time but it's doubtful Fitzroy's loss had any impact on her personally and in fact, his loss strengthened Mary's position and removed a rival to Jane's future children.

Henry Fitzroy, Duke of Richmond and Somerset, c. 1533/4 by Lucas Horenbout, Henry's illegitimate son with his mistress Elizabeth 'Bessie' Blount; there was a possibility that Henry was considering making him his heir but his early death put paid to any plans he had.

Jane focused her attention on Mary's impending arrival at court, quietly encouraging Henry who had reinstated his daughter's household and who appeared to look forward to his daughter's arrival. Sometime in the autumn Mary arrived at the palace splendidly dressed and was received by her father and Jane in front of the entire Tudor court. She curtsied upon entering the room and then approached the couple before falling to her knees and asking her father's blessing which he gladly gave, and, helping her to her feet, he kissed his wife and daughter.

In a horror-inducing moment Henry turned on his court stating, 'some of you weare desirous that I should have put this jewell to death.' Whether he was trying to shift the blame for his actions or even playing mind games to remind his daughter of what peril she had been in, Jane quickly stepped in, saying 'that had been great pittie to have lost your chefest jewell of England'.[17] This quick thinking appeared to rescue the situation as Henry turned to Jane smiling and, putting a hand on her stomach, said 'nay Edward, Edward'. It was too much for Mary who fell into a dead faint, greatly worrying both the king and queen. When she recovered Henry, letting his parental instincts take over, held her hand and walked up and down with her, reassuring her that she was now safe.

This is the first concrete mention of the possibility of a child for Henry and Jane but we know Jane would not give birth until October 1537; if she went to term, the earliest she could have been pregnant was January 1537 and, even then, she wouldn't have been sure until a few months later. Did Jane suffer a miscarriage in 1536? Apart from Henry's comment, we have no surviving evidence that she was pregnant but if she had been and had lost the child, there is little doubt Henry and Jane would have covered it up: heir-wise, England was in a precarious situation as it was, and they wouldn't have been able to afford another failure. Also, if Jane had suffered a miscarriage, why did Henry stand by her? Was it too soon to get rid of another wife? It hadn't seemed to have bothered him earlier in the year and he had proved that he could quickly move on to the next woman he desired.

My belief is that Henry was expressing his hope that Jane was pregnant or that she would be soon, not that they knew she was at this time; it was his ultimate hope and wish for the future but he was having doubts about it. In a somewhat risky conversation in August 1536, Cromwell told Chapuys that Henry had confided to him that he doubted he would be able to have children with Jane. This is an unusually frank admission from the king, even more so when you take into account that when Chapuys had told him on a previous occasion there was no guarantee of male children from any future wife, Henry had exploded with rage. Also, why did Cromwell confide this to Chapuys? Henry did not like his private business being the subject of gossip and Chapuys was the ambassador of Henry's sometime friend/rival Charles V. Were both Henry and Cromwell playing games with the ambassador or was it a rare moment of self-reflection on Henry's part? Cromwell was a man who thought through everything; if Henry had confided his fears to him, he would have immediately considered what that meant for England, and at that point Mary would have been the only viable heir. Perhaps with this conversation he was laying the groundwork for her future accession if it was needed and giving one of her biggest allies and someone he could work with, a heads-up. Even so, it was still a risky move.

An adaptation of the Whitehall Mural by Remigius van Leemput, year unknown. The future Edward VI is included this time.

It is interesting to note that he referred to their future son as Edward too; the future Edward VI was born on 12 October 1537 and it was believed he was so named because he was born on the eve of the feast day of St Edward the Confessor, but perhaps there was another more emotional reason at play. Henry had lost two named sons so far: Henry Duke of Cornwall and Henry Duke of Richmond, so perhaps the name Henry had become too painful for him to contemplate.

Mary and Jane settled into an easy, close relationship. They both shared similar interests and were both conservative in religion, and they were also close in age so perhaps Jane acted as more of an older sister to Mary than a stepmother. They were often seen walking in hand in hand; Jane was determined to keep Mary with her whenever she could and always treated her with respect. Perhaps the best thing Jane did for Mary apart from helping reunite her with her father is that she never tried to replace Catherine. In the words of Lauren Mackay from her book *Inside the Tudor Court: Henry VIII and His Six Wives Through the Writings of the Spanish Ambassador Eustace Chapuys*: 'Anne had invited her to call her "mother"; Jane had taken it as a given that Katherine would always be irreplaceable in her daughter eyes.'[18]

One person who is missing from this scene is the newly titled Lady Elizabeth, daughter of Henry and Anne Boleyn. Elizabeth had not yet turned 3 but she was old enough to understand her change of status, questioning her governor as to why she was no longer referred to as 'my lady princess'. The argument can be made that she was too young to be at court but she had previously attended and had been shown off on important occasions; the truth was it was too painful, too awkward and too soon to have her there. Her mother had just been executed as a traitor and Henry did not want any reminders of Anne or her downfall around him; in fact, he was well on his way to wiping her from history.

For Jane there would have been a degree of awkwardness and guilt; whatever she may have believed about Anne's 'crimes', a young girl had lost her mother and now Jane, who had risen thanks to her fall, was taking her place. Until recently it was believed Jane only had the barest contact with Elizabeth but Sylvia Barbara Soberton has found evidence that Jane actually paid more attention to Elizabeth than first thought. In *Rival Sisters: Mary and Elizabeth Tudor* Soberton reveals that an inventory known as 'A Book of the Queen's Jewels' which lists Jane's valuables and the gifts she gave, shows records of Jane giving both Mary and Elizabeth beads, pomanders and girdles. Another account shows she provided Elizabeth with clothing and linen from the Queen's Wardrobe and paid for a New Year's gift for her. Jane was not uncaring of Elizabeth but circumstances made their relationship difficult and she would always be closer to Mary whom she had so much in common with.[19]

Jane could look back on her first few months of queenship with a degree of satisfaction; she had helped Henry and Mary reunite, built a stronger relationship with Mary herself, greeted ambassadors, assembled her household and had been widely accepted by the people

The future Elizabeth I as a princess, c. 1546/7 possibly by William Scrots. Whilst Jane did not have as close a relationship with Elizabeth as she did with Mary, she did not neglect her. Evidence survives of payments and gifts to Henry's younger daughter.

of England. She was not pregnant but there was still time, and for the moment everything was going as well she could have hoped for … but trouble was brewing.

The irony of Jane being religiously conservative stands in contrast to the most obvious destruction of parts of her faith during her queenship: the dissolution of the monasteries was about to begin. Jane had hoped her marriage to Henry would help bring about a return to the old ways and at first there were high hopes that this would happen. Henry at heart was also a conservative but had been forced to work with reformers and adapt new policies and methods when the Pope had refused to allow him to divorce Catherine of Aragon. With both Catherine and Anne gone and a new conservative queen on the throne, it was rather naively thought that there was no reason things couldn't go back to the way they had been before.

However, Henry had grown tired of outside interference and after such great effort to gain control of the Church in England, he wasn't about to surrender it. He firmly believed the Pope had usurped the position and rights that were meant to be his and knew that there was backing for reform as there had been complaints of church abuses for a number of years. Henry now wanted to establish a Church that reflected what Henry himself believed.

At first not a lot changed. Henry instead of the Pope was now regarded as head of the Church but this would not have made a massive difference to the everyday man and woman in England. However, the reformers wanted to go further; they believed in justification by faith alone rather than good works and wanted to stop the veneration of relics, prayers for the dead and to the Saints, the Mass, the Sacraments and going on pilgrimage, as they were, at best, superstitious ploys and idolatrous at worst.

There was also discussion surrounding the possibility of the bible being printed in English so everyone could read and understand the word of the Lord. In an attempt to clarify matters and find a middle ground between the reformers and the conservatives, Henry established the Ten Articles in July 1536. These were adopted by clerical convocation and were:

1. That Holy Scriptures and the three Creeds are the basis and summary of a true Christian faith.
2. That baptism conveys remission of sins and the regenerating grace of the Holy Spirit, and is absolutely necessary as well for children as adults.
3. That penance consists of contrition, confession, and reformation, and is necessary to salvation.
4. That the body and blood of Christ are really present in the elements of the eucharist.
5. That justification is remission of sin and reconciliation to God by the merits of Christ; but good works are necessary.
6. That images are useful as remembrancers, but are not objects of worship.
7. That saints are to be honoured as examples of life, and as furthering our prayers.
8. That saints may be invoked as intercessors, and their holy days observed.
9. That ceremonies are to be observed for the sake of their mystical signification, and as conducive to devotion.

10. That prayers for the dead are good and useful, but the efficacy of papal pardon, and of soul-masses offered at certain localities, is negatived.[20]

These Articles must have come as a disappointment to the pro-Catholic faction and Jane herself; we can see the attempt to introduce a middle way between the opposing factions, something that would be more successful under Elizabeth, but they left many people confused and unhappy as not being Catholic or reformed enough.

The monasteries were the next to be examined; as Henry aged, he appeared to take an increasing dislike of monastic buildings and activities, or perhaps it was simply because the monasteries were a very visual reminder of Rome opposing him? The monasteries had been a part of English life for hundreds of years; they were a familiar and a reassuring presence to the people but they could have become a source of future trouble and defiance against Henry. However, the wholescale destruction that was about to start was excessive, almost emanating from pathological hatred.

The ruins of St Mary's Abbey, York. St Mary's was one of the wealthiest and most powerful monasteries in England. (Author's Collection)

Closeup of the damage to St Mary's Abbey. Whilst some has been caused by nature and time, some was committed at the time of its dissolution. Statues were torn down, stained-glass windows were smashed and the buildings themselves were destroyed; the bricks were often reused elsewhere. Jane was horrified at the dissolution of the monasteries and made efforts to save some but was ultimately unsuccessful. (*Author's Collection*)

The second item of interest to note is that the monasteries were filled with vast wealth. Pilgrims and donations arrived from all over the country and the rich often left a portion of their wealth to the Church in their wills. Henry and England were desperately short of money. Henry had inherited a vast treasury when he became king thanks to his father's wise prudent dealings but that money was virtually all gone.

Cromwell, as Vicar-General, launched an investigation into the state of monasticism in England in 1535, sending commissioners to each and every house in England; over a year later he had compiled his report and it made for damning reading. It revealed that the commissioners had found evidence of 'loose living', that some priors visited whores, some had long-term lovers that they had had children with and there were affairs between nuns and priors. Corruption and misuse of donations were common and 'relics' from saints were proved to be false and used to con innocent people out of their money, and gambling was also a frequent activity.

The Act for the Dissolution of the Monasteries was passed just before Easter 1536 and allowed the king to take control of smaller monasteries that were worth less than £200 a year. Soon after his marriage to Jane, the process of stripping and selling off these smaller institutions began; anything that could be sold, be it materials or goods, was. A small portion of the money was given to those who suddenly found themselves homeless whilst the rest went straight to the royal treasury. If they did not accept a pension, the men and woman who had lived in the monasteries were transferred to larger houses nearby.

Whilst it can be believed that there were some houses filled with corruption and vice, there were equally those that were good and valuable assets to their community. The nunnery at Catesby was one such property where Cromwell's commissioners were reportedly impressed with the 'wyse and discreete' prioress and the behaviour of her nuns; there were no signs of lewd behaviour here and all the nuns were regarded as devout and religious; the nunnery was also noted to be of great benefit to the local community and the commissioners actually encouraged the king and Cromwell to let this institute remain. Jane was closely involved in the negotiations undertaken to save Catesby and even offered to buy the property as revealed in a surviving letter from the prioress:

Pleaseth it your mastership to call to your remembrance that doctor Gwent informed you yesternight that the queen's grace hath moved the king's majesty for me, and hath offered his highness two thousand marks in recompence of that house of Catesby, and hath as yet no perfect answer. If it may like you now, in my great sorrow and pensiveness, to be so good master to me as to obtain that the king's grace do grant that the house may stand, and get me years of payment for the two thousand marks, you shall have a hundred marks of me to buy you a gelding, and my prayers during my life, and all my sisters during their lives. I trust you have not forgotten the report that the commissioners did send unto you of me and my sisters. Master Onley saith that he hath a grant of the house; but my very trust is in God and you to help forward that the queen's grace may obtain her request that it may stand. And thus I beseech Almighty God send you ever such comfort as your need, as it was to my heart yesternight, when Dr Gwent did send me word that you would move the King's grace for me this morning again.[21]

To Jane's disappointment this good and glorious house would not survive, neither would many others. Elizabeth Norton has found evidence that Jane tried, indirectly this time, to save another house, a nunnery at Clementhorpe in Yorkshire. This time it was her household officers that were approached by a man called Christopher Ascue. The discussion took place in the Queen's Chamber at Windsor Castle so it must be assumed that if Jane wasn't there (when Ascue was later examined by the king's council, he does not mention her presence), she was at least aware of what her officers were doing and that Ascue thought it was worth speaking to her or them. Both men promised to ask Jane to intercede for the nunnery but sadly it was to be another failure for her, and the nunnery had closed by the end of 1536.[22]

Thomas Howard, 3rd Duke of Norfolk by Hans Holbein the Younger, c. 1539. Norfolk would be one of two men responsible for organising Jane's funeral; he had to look back to Elizabeth of York's funeral in 1503 in order to ensure everything was done correctly.

Whilst Jane deeply regretted the loss of the monasteries and her lack of ability to save them, she may have received some 'gifts' from them. When the gold was seized from a shrine at Bridlington by the Duke of Norfolk, he thought of the queen, writing to Henry: 'be a thief I would have stolen them to have sent to the Queen's grace, but now your Highness having them may give unto her without offence.'[23] It's not known if Jane ever actually received this 'gift' but it is interesting that Norfolk thought she would like it, unless he was simply trying to buy favour with his queen. Jane may have reasoned that if she didn't accept it, someone else would.

Jane was not the only one who was unhappy with the closure of the monasteries – the people were too. Cromwell's commissioners did state that some were of much benefit to their area and even the ones that were discovered to have been less reputable may have still provided an invaluable service to their community; nothing is ever truly black and white. The monasteries helped the poor and sick, provided a place to stay for a weary traveller, performed acts of charity alongside many other duties. Taking them away left a massive shortfall in support for the community affected and tensions soon started to boil over.

When the commissioners travelled to Hexham to begin the dissolution of the monastery there, they heard that the monks had taken steps to defend themselves and as they approached, they heard the bells tolling and found the gates closed to them. One of the monks then informed them that they would die before they surrendered their house to them, and finding no other way to enter, the commissioners were forced to retreat. No one knew it then but things were about to get much worse.

In October, the Vicar of Louth was informed that the commissioners were on their way to his church, and in his next sermon he angrily denounced them to his congregation. Following the service, the townspeople walked in procession behind the church's three silver crosses to mark the first Sunday after Michaelmas when a yeoman called Thomas Foster declared: 'go we to follow the crosses for and if they be taken from us, we be like to follow them no more.'[24]

The townspeople quickly decided the crosses had to be protected at all costs. After the procession they were returned to their rightful place and the keys were removed from the churchwarden to better ensure no one could take them away. Soon after they learned that an official of the Bishop of Lincoln had arrived in Louth to select the town's officials. The

The Mortimer panther displaying the impaled arms of Henry VIII and Jane Seymour (part of the king's beasts at the entrance of Hampton Court Palace). (*Author's Collection*)

man, John Henneage, was seized by the crowd and forced to swear that he would be true to God, the king and the commonalty; they finished with him by burning his books but at least he was allowed to go unharmed. Around sixty parish priests were also forced to swear the oath.

Slightly unluckier were two servants of Cromwell's, Johns Bellowe and Milsent, who were captured and imprisoned for a time, and it was this that alerted Henry, Jane and the court to the trouble brewing. At first, they were told that the two men had been brutally murdered by the crowd; thankfully, this was later discovered to be untrue, but events were now escalating. A crowd of around 20,000 had assembled and now marched from Louth to Caister where Lord Burgh, assisted by commissioners, was about to start collecting the king's tax subsidy. When the people of Caister heard the news of the approaching crowd, they rose up as well, telling the commissioners they would pay them no more. They then started ringing the bells to raise the alarm. The commissioners sensibly tried to flee but some were captured whilst others raced to inform the king of the escalating situation.

The rebels, as they were now referred, were able to recruit noblemen to their cause but how willingly these men came is debatable. Whilst there was a lot of sympathy for the rebels' complaints, and some may have joined the cause genuinely of their own free will, others may have been 'persuaded' by threats and blackmail. This was true of Lord Latimer, whose wife Catherine Parr and his children were held by the rebels to ensure his compliance.

The Pilgrimage of Grace 1536, by an unknown artist, c. nineteenth century. The rebels or pilgrims always maintained they were loyal to their king; it was his ministers they believed were ruining the country.

By 4 October the numbers had swelled to 40,000 and Henry realised he had a full-blown rebellion on his hands. He planned to confront them himself and started assembling troops and arms and appointed Jane regent in his absence. This little-known fact is often overlooked but there is a surviving list of men appointed to serve Jane and counsel her during this difficult time, which proves that Jane was not an empty-headed symbol who did as she was told when she was told. She would not have had the experience and knowledge of Catherine of Aragon and would rely on councillors more than Catherine, but the fact that she was made regent at all was a significant honour and vote of confidence in her abilities.[25] However, the situation deteriorated further and Henry had second thoughts, deciding to stay behind and command from a distance.

Soon after, Henry and Jane received a list of demands from the rebels and Henry was furious to read that they were trying to dictate to him. Amongst the known demands was the restoration of the Church's old ways and the monasteries to be left unmolested; they also wanted Cranmer and Cromwell removed and punished, believing they were the source of much of the heresies in the kingdom and demanded that nobles be appointed as his counsellors.

Henry wrote a scathing response:

Concerning choosing of Counsellors, I never have read, heard, nor known that prince's counsellors and prelates should be appointed by rude and ignorant common people; nor that they were persons meet, or of ability, to discern and chose meet and sufficient counsellors for a prince. How presumptuous then are ye, the rude commons of one shire, and that one of the most brute and beastly of the whole realm, and of least experience, to find fault with your Prince for the electing of his counsellors and prelates; and to take upon you, contrary to God's law and man's law, to rule your Prince, whom ye are bound by all laws to obey and serve, with both your lives, lands and goods, and for no worldly cause to withstand: the contrary whereof you, like traitors and rebels, have attempted, and not like true subjects, as ye name yourselves.[26]

Gone was his famous charm and common touch, and with so many gathered this looks to be a foolhardy response but it does give us an indication of Henry's true state of mind and character at the time and perhaps his character in future. However, the rebels always claimed they had no quarrel with the king and remained his loyal subjects – it was just his bad advisors they were angry with. When they received this angry response, the crowd did climb down somewhat, perhaps instinctually responding to their love and loyalty for their king.

In the same letter Henry criticised their demands for the restoration of the Church and monasteries as they once were, and here he was on much firmer ground: there were abuses and corruption and those houses did need to be reformed or closed. Henry pointed this out but failed to mention that even good and virtuous houses were potentially in danger. He also correctly pointed out that he had done nothing that was not consented to by Parliament and the spiritual and temporal nobles of England.

With the rebels now backing down, Henry and Jane probably thought the crisis was over but they were about to be rudely confronted with a similar-sized rebellion in Lincolnshire. Led by a lawyer named Robert Aske, this uprising was better organised and commanded and grew to be as large as its predecessor. Aske also denied he was rebelling against his king and called himself and his followers pilgrims, stating: 'would have it call'd yet only a Pilgrimage of Grace, while, for giving it reputation, certain priests with crosses led the way, the army following with banners, wherein were painted the crucifix, the five wounds and the chalice.'[27]

The Pilgrimage of Grace would be the name this rebellion would always be known as; the pilgrims walked under a banner depicting the five Holy wounds of Jesus Christ to show their cause was religious and for God.

Jane watched these events with concern – for herself, her husband

A banner bearing the Holy Wounds of Jesus Christ was carried during the Pilgrimage of Grace. (*Wikipedia*)

and the people of England. As a traditional Catholic she sympathised and agreed with many of points the rebels made but she was also Henry's wife and queen and like so many of the nobles around her, stood between two opposing mighty forces. But her conscience was troubling her and it forced her to make her only known political act during her entire reign.

Approaching Henry publicly, Jane fell to her knees before him and begged him to restore the abbeys. Jane's sympathies were well known but no one had expected so blatant a demonstration of them. She perhaps thought, with a sympathetic audience surrounding them, Henry would see the logic of her plea and her action as part of her role as queen to act as an intercessor for others. She probably tried to speak up in private but failed and with the old ways and the monasteries being such a key part of her faith, wanted to try and preserve them and keep Henry on what she genuinely believed was the right path. She ventured to say that perhaps God had permitted the rebellion in response to the destruction of the churches and monasteries. Such brazenness from the normally reserved, conforming queen surprised the court but it infuriated her husband.

Henry angrily told her to get up off her knees and not to meddle in his affairs; he then reminded her of Anne Boleyn's fate which must have inspired instant terror. If Jane had suspected Anne had not been guilty as charged, then she now got a more direct hint that there had been other reasons for her destruction. Like Anne, Jane was not a secure woman. All she had was Henry's love to sustain her and her marriage; they had not even produced a child as yet – she could easily be got rid of with little trouble and there would be no one to help her.[28]

Henry did not like to be contradicted and he did not like to be told he was wrong, especially in public. It is a sign of the strength and determination of Jane's beliefs and character that she was willing to take such a dramatic step. However, unlike Anne, who would have pushed and argued her point, Jane knew when to back down and this is what she did. Nothing could be gained from antagonising Henry further; in fact, a great deal could be lost, so she backed down and retreated to the domestic side of her role as queen. This was not a cowardly act, it was a sensible one; when she had a son or circumstances improved, she could always try again.

For a while, circumstances did not improve, the rebels took York and then Hull, reopening the monasteries and admitting the nuns and

Etching of the Pilgrimage of Grace 1536, by Fred Kirk Shaw, c. 1913. The Pilgrimage of Grace was the most serious threat Henry faced during his reign.

monks once again. Their numbers grew with each city they arrived at and in the end surpassed the numbers of the previous rebellion with over 40,000 people marching under the banner; meanwhile the royal forces numbered less than 15,000. Faced with this enormous threat, an angry Henry had no choice but to negotiate with the rebels. Authorising the Duke of Norfolk to act on his behalf, on 26 October, the duke met with Aske to negotiate a truce. The demands were familiar and this may be why by the 28th, Norfolk and Aske had come to an agreement with Henry signing a general pardon for all offences committed before 1 November.

Henry was still angry that he had been forced to give in to their demands but put on a good face, for the time being – like Jane, but in wildly different circumstances and for different reasons, he was waiting for the right moment to act. The truce held and having got their pardon, the rebels started to disperse. Henry invited Aske to spend Christmas at Greenwich Palace. When he arrived, Henry was at his affable best, even gifting him a jacket of crimson silk. Henry told him he planned to soon come on Progress to York and that Jane could perhaps be crowned in York Minster. For Aske who had never witnessed Henry's anger or his ability to mask it, this news could not have pleased him more and he

York Minster. Henry told Robert Aske that it was possible Jane would be crowned there.

never suspected that Henry was deceiving him and waiting for a chance to exact revenge.

What did Jane think watching this display? She was probably fearful as she would have known Henry was playing a part and she was unsure exactly what was coming; maybe Henry's actions sickened her but we can only suggest this with the benefit of hindsight. Perhaps she had her mind on other things. On 21 December her father, Sir John, died aged about 60. We don't know how close they were; he did not receive any benefits when she became queen but this means little: he was still her father and the loss will have been great. As royal custom dictated, Jane did not attend his funeral and in fact would have been needed at court for the Christmas celebrations. Sir John was first laid to rest in the church of Eastern Priory but following the deterioration and later collapse of the building, he was disinterred in 1590 by his grandson Edward Seymour, Earl of Hertford, and reburied in St Mary's Church, Great Bedwyn, the parish church of Wulfhall which he would have known so well. His monument can still be seen today.[29]

Once Christmas was over, Aske departed and returned to the North, telling his followers of his faith and trust in the king and described Henry as a 'gracious sovereign lord'. Sadly, for Aske and others, trouble would be brewing once again in the North a couple of months later.

One man who was not convinced Henry's promises were genuine was a Sir Francis Bigod. Whilst he was correct, his actions provided Henry with the excuse he had been waiting for. Over February and March 1537, a handful of smaller rebellions broke out and Bigod attempted to retake Hull. As the truce had been broken by the rebels, Henry had no need to honour his own promises that had been made under duress; it didn't matter that most of the people originally involved were no longer so and in Aske's case he even attempted to put down these smaller rebellions, Henry reacted decisively. The Duke of Norfolk was ordered to put down the rebellions and he succeeded; the Pilgrimage of Grace was over and soon after the arrests, the executions started. Bigod was hanged at Tyburn whilst Aske was hanged, still alive, in chains from Clifford's Tower, the Keep of York Castle. It would have taken him several days to die. In total 216 people were executed for their part in the rebellion; the guilty ranged from lords and knights to abbots, monks and parish priests.[30]

One of the men executed, Sir Robert Constable, was a distant relative of Jane's on her mother's side. Constable wrote to his son begging him to ask Jane to plead for his life; whether Jane received the petition or not is unknown but there was very little she could have done anyway. Henry was determined that those who had crossed him would pay, horrifically. Like Aske, Constable was hanged alive in chains at Hull.[31]

A history of Clifford's Tower showing the year of Robert Aske's execution. (*Author's Collection*)

By the end of March 1537, the rebellion was over, and all that was left to do was clear up the loose ends. We are left with the

Clifford's Tower. Robert Aske was hung in chains whilst still alive from this tower; it would not have been a quick death. (*Author's Collection*)

question: would Henry have retaliated if the smaller rebellions hadn't broken out? I think he would but would have been forced to appear as if he was responding to something else. Henry could not stand to be told he was wrong and that he shouldn't do this or that and, as king, he believed he should not be contradicted – he was God' s appointed representative. He would have found a way or an excuse to punish the rebels for their actions in 1536, no matter what.

Copy of the Whitehall Mural by Remigius van Leemput, c. 1667. The original painted by Hans Holbein the Younger showed Henry VII and Elizabeth of York standing behind Henry VIII and Jane Seymour and displayed the Tudor dynasty as Henry VIII saw it; it's possible Jane was pregnant when it was painted. The mural was destroyed by fire in 1698.

What about Jane? After her failed intervention, what did she think of the matter? What did she think of her husband's actions towards Aske? It takes a certain kind of person to act as a friend to an enemy; not all of us have it in us. Henry went so far as to give Aske gifts and spoke publicly of him and appeared friendly, all the while hating him. Jane knew this, she would have witnessed and heard Henry's anger in private. Perhaps he even vented directly to her; she would have known Henry was waiting for a chance to retaliate. Did she try to warn Aske? Probably not – too many eyes were on the Queen of England, including her husband's and she had already been thoroughly rebuffed when attempting to intercede on the political front. That's not to say she didn't feel sympathy or concern for Aske and the others, but like with her relative Constable, she was powerless in this situation.

This was a frightening time for Jane. Whilst she was not as vocal as her predecessor, she was known to be for the old ways; she also partially agreed with the rebels' cause. But after her public stand, was she put under surveillance? A queen was in the public eye and her every action and word was dissected and reported back to every interested party anyway but now that she had presented herself 'obviously' for the rebels, like Mary before her, could she have become some sort of focal point? We have no surviving evidence to suggest this and Jane did take Henry's firm response as a warning and retreated, but was it enough? Cromwell had eyes and ears everywhere and it would have been foolish of him not to at least monitor Jane during this troublesome time.

Jane Seymour by Hans Holbein the Younger, c. 1536.

Reprisals, punishments and executions would continue into May 1537 but they weren't the focus of people's attention anymore, not even Henry's. In May 1537, after nearly a year of marriage, it was confirmed that Queen Jane was pregnant.[32 & 33]

Chapter 8

Triumph and Disaster

Quite when Jane suspected she was pregnant we'll never know; expectant mothers knew in Tudor times that a pregnancy lasted nine months but they had no way of accurately confirming it until the baby started to move in the womb; however, there would have been signs. Some women become sensitive to smell and taste, a once-favoured food could become a much-hated dish to be avoided; they can suffer from increasing fatigue and nausea and physically they may start to experience tenderness or swelling in their breasts and stop having their period. These signs could be an indication of illness too.

Whilst announcing nothing publicly, Jane did confide her suspicions to Henry and her physician. We know this because Henry wrote to Norfolk of Jane's suspected pregnancy in March 1537, to which the duke responded with his hearty congratulations.[1] As with many secrets at a royal court, rumour and suspicions soon started to spread with courtiers gossiping about the possibility and even praying it was so. In a letter written to Honor Grenville, Viscountess Lisle, wife of Arthur Plantagenet, Lord Lisle, (Henry's uncle on his mother's side), John Husee, their agent in London, informed her that there was talk of Jane's pregnancy and that he was heartily praying for a prince.[2] At this time the viscountess was trying to place her daughters in Jane's household so this information would have been put to good use in future persuasions. Henry's council also discussed the pregnancy when they met at Westminster at the beginning of April.

Finally in May, the baby 'quickened', which meant that the baby had moved for the first time and Jane, Henry and the people of England now knew she was definitely pregnant, hopefully with the future king of England. In another auspicious sign the baby quickened on 27 May which that year was Trinity Sunday. Trinity Sunday celebrates the Christian doctrine of the Trinity or the three persons of God: the Father, the Son and the Holy Spirit. Now that there was no doubt, Jane's pregnancy was finally announced to the public; in London the chronicler Charles Wriothesley recorded the occasion:

> Alsoe the 27th daye of Maye 1537, being Trynytie Sondaye, there was Te Deum sounge in Powles for joye of the Queenes quickninge of childe, my Lord Chaunseler, Lord Privaye Seale, with diverse other Lordes and Bishopps, beinge then present; the Mayre and Aldermen with the beste craftes of the cyttye beinge there in their lyveryes, all gevinge laude and prayse to God for joye of the same, wher the Bishopp of Worcester, called Docter Latymer, made an oration afore all the Lordes and Commons, after Te Deum was songe, shewinge the cause of their assemblye, which oration was mervelouse fruitefull to the hearers; and alsoe the same night was diverse greate fyers made in London … [and] a hogshead of wyne at everye fyer for poore people to drinke as longe as yt woulde laste; I praye Jesue, and it be his will, send us a Prince.[3]

The stained-glass window at Hampton Court Palace showing Jane Seymour's descent from Edward I and III. (*Author's Collection*)

Closeup of Jane's badge as queen from the stained-glass window at Hampton Court depicting her descent from Edward I and III. (*Author's Collection*)

All over England the people rejoiced and celebrations broke out. At York, in a rare display of generosity, the Duke of Norfolk gave four of his own hogsheads of wine to the people of the city and ordered a *Te Deum* to be sung and bonfires lit. In Oxford this sermon was preached:

> The last and greatest benefit, the special cause of their assembly, is 'that our most excellent lady and mistress queen Jane, our noble and godly prince's, King Henry the Eighth's, wife, hath conceived and is great with child, and upon Trinity Sunday, like one given of God, the child quickened in the mother's womb'. Exhorts them to give praise, and pray that it may be a prince.[4]

The excitement of Jane's pregnancy would only be surpassed by the actual birth. Henry and England had waited a long time for a prince; there had been multiple pregnancies that had resulted in losses (or princesses) and after so long all Henry wanted was surety and so did his people; a prince would finally be the uncontested heir to the throne but they would have to wait and see.

For Jane the excitement mingled with the practical. She was soon adding panels to her dresses or wearing open-laced gowns to accommodate her increasing size. Like many women before and after, she also developed cravings, specifically quails and cucumbers. Mary was able to assist her stepmother with the cucumber cravings as she had them sent to Jane from her own garden; however, the quails were slightly more problematic, Jane just couldn't seem to get enough of them.

Henry couldn't do enough for Jane now that she was pregnant and the concerned and doting husband immediately set about catering for her heart's desire. It is amusing to think of the powerful King Henry VIII of England desperately trying to source quails for his pregnant wife. When the sources in England proved unsatisfactory, Henry was forced to look abroad. An apparently harassed Sir John Rusell asked Lord Lisle's agent John Hussee to write to his master and speed things along:

> Sir John Russell, called me unto him, and asked me when I heard from your lordship, saying further that he had these days past wrote unto your lordship in sundry letters by the king's commandment expressly, and how the very effect of those letters was for fat quails for

the queen's highness, which her Grace loveth very well, and longeth not a little for them; and he looked hourly for your lordship's answer with the said quails, in so much that he did further command me in the king's behalf to write your lordship with all haste expressly again for the said quails.[5]

The painted spotted Seymour panther in the recreated Tudor Garden at Hampton Court Palace. (*Author's Collection*)

Alongside a new wave of affection and adoration from her husband, he also relaxed his guard and included her more in foreign policy. The emperor sent a new ambassador to negotiate a marriage for Mary and the King of Portugal's brother and Jane took part in discussions for the match. Charles V clearly thought that Jane was worth cultivating and had influence as he instructed the ambassador to assure her that Mary's intended would prove a good son to her.[6]

A portrait miniature of a young man, perhaps Gregory Cromwell by Hans Holbein the Younger, c. 1543. The only son of Thomas Cromwell, he was Jane's brother-in-law by virtue of his marriage to her sister Elizabeth.

Whilst enjoying this newfound influence, Jane was more than aware that everything rested on her pregnancy and her ability to deliver a healthy son so she took every precaution she could to ensure a successful outcome. She attended few engagements during this time, even missing her younger sister's wedding. Elizabeth's husband, Sir Anthony Ughtred, had died in October 1534 and Elizabeth had been left to raise two children. She ran into difficulties and by March 1537 was writing to Cromwell asking for his assistance, and whilst Elizabeth was probably hoping to be granted some property, Cromwell seized the opportunity of securing a good match for his only son and heir, Gregory. He suggested the marriage to Elizabeth and by June 1537 she had accepted, they were married on 3 August 1537 at Mortlake.

It is interesting that we have no surviving evidence that Elizabeth wrote to her sister the queen for assistance. It's possible the letters have been lost or perhaps the sisters were not that close. It's worth taking into consideration that both sisters served Catherine and Anne when they were queen, but Jane remained devoted to Catherine and Mary whilst Elizabeth's husband was a Boleyn supporter who greatly benefitted from Anne's rise, receiving both promotions and property. It's possible there was a certain distance between the two at this time following the bloody events of May 1536.

Jane settled into a quiet a life as possible at court and focused on her household. When a space became available and remembering Lord Lisle's efforts to secure quails for her, Jane showed how grateful she was by agreeing to take one of the viscountess's daughters. The sisters, Catherine and Anne Bassett, resided in Calais with their mother and stepfather so they were sent over for Jane to inspect and interview personally. Jane had high standards and she expected the people serving her to meet and maintain them, a sign that she took her mother's early lessons and tutelage to heart and in fact did her proud. Flirtatious

Jane or Joan, Lady Meutas by Hans Holbein the Younger, c. 1536–43. A lady in Jane's Privy Chamber.

behaviour had reached its height in Anne's court but there was never a breath of scandal surrounding Jane's. John Husee wrote a detailed letter to Viscountess Lisle warning her of what Jane expected:

> And for as much as they shall now go upon making and marring, it shall please your ladyship to exhort them to be sober, sad, wise and discreet, and lowly above all things, and to be obedient, and governed and ruled by my lady of Rutland and my lady Sussex, and Mrs Margery and such others as be your ladyship's friend here; and to serve God and to be virtuous, for that is much regarded, to serve God well, and to be sober of tongue.[7]

Jane knew that the behaviour of her ladies would reflect on her and her reputation and she had no desire to become a laughing stock or nourish a rival for her husband's affections. To this end she made sure they were dressed strictly according to her specifications too. Jane always favoured the more modest English gable hood than the daring French hood, and once she became queen that was one of the first things to disappear; it can also be seen as a careful and deliberate contrast to her predecessor as Henry had been heard to say he was tired of French fashions and ways.

Even before the two girls arrived, Jane required them to have two sets of clothes, one of satin and the other of damask and 'good attirements for the head and neck'.[8] Unfortunately, both arrived dressed in the French fashion. Anne would be the lucky girl chosen to serve Jane and initially it was agreed she could wear out her French dress but Jane soon changed her mind and commanded Anne to dress appropriately when she appeared before her.

Whilst she was strict with her ladies, Jane's surviving portraiture shows us that she herself dressed splendidly, as befitted Henry's wife and queen, but she may have loved fashion, beautiful clothes and fabrics for their own sake and as queen was able to indulge on a much grander scale than before. Sir John Russell famously noted 'that the richer she [Jane] was in apparel, the fairer and goodly lady she was and appeared; and the other [Anne] was the contrary, for the richer she was apparelled, the worse she looked.'[9] Jane is portrayed wearing beautiful jewellery, and some of it will have been made specifically for her but some would have come from the 'Queen's jewels'. The 'Queen's jewels' were items inherited by every queen of England from her predecessor and were extremely valuable. As with all areas of fashion, styles changed and some of the jewellery may have fallen from regular use as time went on but others could be (and were) readapted. The most notable 'recycling' though appears to be a necklace worn by Jane, now sometimes called the 'Consort's necklace'. The same necklace appears in a portrait believed to be of Catherine Howard and later in one of Catherine Parr though it

Queen Jane Seymour by Hans Holbein the Younger, c. 1536/7. This portrait is probably the most instantly recognised image of Jane.

has undergone significant alterations by the time of the last Catherine's tenure as queen.

For all her precautions Jane could not control everything, as in the summer of 1537 there was another outbreak of the sweating sickness, a disease that could kill within hours and infected anyone whether they were healthy or unhealthy, male or female, young or old. Along with the usual pressures and anxieties she was already trying to manage, the sickness was a most unwelcome extra. Whilst Henry was notoriously afraid of sickness and indeed during the summer of 1537 took his own precautions, he was not as noticeably affected as Jane, but he didn't quite have as much riding on her pregnancy as Jane did. Even people not close to her were able to pick up on her fears. Sir John Russell wrote at this time to Cromwell:

After I had received your letter, immediately I went to the King, then going to supper, and showed his Majesty your misfortune in the sickness of Bold, your servant. His Grace was sorry and answered there was no danger, but that you might repair to Court in a day or two. Thereupon he told the Queen, who I perceived was afraid, whereupon, considering that her Grace is with child, and the case that she is in, I went again to the King and said I perceived the Queen was afraid. His Majesty answered that the Queen was somewhat afraid, but that ye might lie at Mr. Westone's, Mr. Browne's, my lord Marquis', and other good fellows' houses, and meet his Grace daily at hunting and keep him company all day till night, for the present.[10]

Russell was not the only one to notice. John Husee also wrote to Viscountess Lisle: 'Your Ladyship would not believe how much the Queen is afraid of the sickness.'[11]

To Henry's credit he took Jane's concerns on board and asked Cromwell to keep away from the court. Jane grew so concerned that she isolated herself at Windsor with a much-reduced household; she didn't accompany Henry on Progress that summer either. Originally this may have had nothing to do with the sickness and more to do with unnecessary stress whilst pregnant but once the sickness started, it was even more imperative she take no unnecessary risks. Henry himself also postponed a trip to the North to re-establish his authority after the failure of the Pilgrimage of Grace. He wrote to the Duke of Norfolk:

Our said most dear and most entirely beloved wife, the queen, now quick with child, for the which we give most humble thanks to Almighty God, albeit she is, in every condition, of that loving inclination, and reverend conformity, that she can in all things well content, satisfy and quiet herself with that thing we shall think expedient and determine; yet considering that, being a woman, upon some sudden and displeasent rumours and bruits that might by foolish or light persons be blown abroad in our absence, being specially so far from her, she might take to her stomach such impressions as might en-gender no little danger or displeasure to that wherewith she is now pregnant, which God forbid; it hath been thought to us and our Council very necessary that for avoiding of all perils that might that way ensue, we should not extend our progress this year so far from her; but direct the same to such place as should not pass 60 miles or thereabouts from her when we should be at the furthest specially she being as it is thought further gone by a month or more than she thought herself at the perfect quickening.[12]

Hampton Court Palace. Jane gave birth to her only child here, the son and heir Henry VIII had destroyed so much to obtain.

By September Jane believed herself to be around a month away from giving birth, so she set about making her final preparations for the birth. She chose Hampton Court Palace for her 'lying in', perhaps because it had recently been renovated. Some of the renovations were specifically requested by Jane herself; in fact a gallery that became known as the

Photo of a part of Hampton Court Palace that looks out onto Clock Court. Jane's chambers look out from the top right window, Jane would not have recognised the magnificent clock we see today as it wasn't installed until 1540, three years after her death. (*Author's Collection*)

'Queen's Gallery' was built on Jane's request, perhaps influenced by the Long Gallery she had known growing up at Wolf Hall. Hampton Court was also outside London which meant less crowds and more fresh air, where hopefully no disease could flourish and as a country girl Jane may have felt and wanted the familiarity and comfort of home – there was quite the landscape surrounding the palace and it may have been a favourite of hers.

'Lying in', 'taking to her chamber' or going into 'confinement' was the occasion the queen officially quit public life for the rest of her pregnancy and retreated to her chambers with only her women for company; no man was allowed to enter, not even the king. Any household duties that were usually performed by men were performed by women for the remaining weeks of the pregnancy. This was not just a routine process; it was a strict ceremonial occasion that had been set down by Henry's own grandmother, Lady Margaret Beaufort, the mother of Henry VII. Margaret had given birth at only 13 and never became pregnant again. Contemporaries and historians today believe giving birth at such a young age did irreparable damage to her health. Margaret may have agreed with them and the rules set out, which became part of the 'Royal Book' on court etiquette, were designed to protect both mother and child in the future.

Once the location had been chosen by the expectant mother, the chambers needed to be prepared to receive her; her rooms were decorated with tapestries and carpets, the ceiling and all windows were to be covered barring one in case the queen wanted a little light. Any cupboards were to be covered and most importantly she would need her bed and a pallet. It is believed the idea of this was to create a womblike environment in order not to shock the newborn baby and also protect the mother from any harm, so everything was covered and 'padded' in order to create a safe environment.

By 16 September everything was prepared. Jane attended Divine Service in the palace's beautiful chapel before she was escorted by the lords and ladies of estate to the Great Chamber which had been splendidly decorated for the occasion. A chair of estate was provided in case she wished to sit, and then she and the guests were served spices and wine. Afterwards Jane was escorted to her chamber where the king, the lords and ladies took their leave of her. She would not emerge until after the birth.

The doorway to Jane Seymour's chambers at Hampton Court, currently closed to the public. Research is being undertaken to see if the chambers can be reopened. (*Author's Collection*)

Henry retired with his household to Esher to await the birth; whilst we might expect him to remain as close to Jane as possible, Esher was not far away and by removing himself and his household, he minimized the risk of exposure to the sickness, which was still circulating.

All through the months leading up to the birth, Jane's pregnancy seems to have progressed well, textbook in fact. All her precautions appear to have paid off and apart from outside interference, she seems to have enjoyed an easy pregnancy so when she felt the first pains of labour on 9 October, she probably expected a relatively easy birth; however, she would be in labour for two days and three nights. Whilst the length of time spent in labour is not set and first-time mothers are usually in labour longer than with the second or third baby, this length of time seems troubling. Was it the first sign that something was wrong? Perhaps the baby wasn't positioned correctly?

By 11 October prayers were being offered for Jane's safe delivery as the chronicler Charles Wriothesley noted:

> This yeare the 11th daie of October, Anno 1537, and the 29th yeare of the raigne of King Henrie the Eight, being Thursdaie, their was a solempne generall procession in London, with all the orders of friars, preistes, and clarkes going all in copes, the major and aldermen, with all the craftes of the cittie, following in their liveries, which was donne to pray for the Queene that was then in labour of chielde.[13]

Perhaps their prayers helped as at 2 o'clock in the morning of 12 October Jane finally gave birth to a healthy child, and, more importantly, the child was a boy.

The euphoria that followed cannot be understated. Henry and England had waited nearly thirty years for a male heir and the celebrations that followed reflected this. A formal procession of thanksgiving was held at St Paul's Cathedral, the *Te Deum* was sung in every parish church and church bells across London rang well into the night. Bonfires were lit, music was played and feasts were held;

Heraldic badge of Queen Jane Seymour as drawn by Thomas Willement.

even the merchants celebrated and gave away fruit, wine and beer to the public. The day ended with a 2,000-gun salute from the Tower of London.

Once Henry heard the good news, he rushed excitedly from Esher to meet his new son and congratulate his wife. After all he'd done (and been through as he would have seen it), he finally had what he most wanted, a son to inherit his kingdom and continue the dynasty.

For Jane, as well as the excitement of meeting her newborn child, there was also the joy of success. She had given birth to a healthy son and she had given England a prince. She couldn't have given Henry a better gift, and all the worries and anxieties she must have felt melted away the minute she held her son in her arms. She was the mother of the future King of England and she was safe, Henry would not set aside or disgrace the mother of his only son and in fact would probably be ready to give her anything she asked for. She and her marriage were completely safe; she had come through this birth so there was a chance of more sons and even daughters to secure the Tudor dynasty.

This was all in the future though. Right now Jane had one last duty to perform before she could rest and recuperate: it was traditionally the queen who announced the birth of a prince or princess and Jane gladly did so. She dictated a letter that was sent to all the lords and ladies of the kingdom and 485 years later we can still hear the pride and joy in her words:

Right trusty and well beloved, we greet you well, and for as much as by the inestimable goodness and grace of Almighty God, we be delivered and brought in childbed of a prince, conceived in most lawful matrimony between my lord the king's majesty and us, doubting not but that for the love and affection which you bear unto us and to the commonwealth of this realm, the knowledge thereof should be joyous and glad tidings unto you, we have thought good to certify you of the same. To the intent you might not only render unto God condign thanks and prayers for so great a benefit but also continually pray for the long continuance and preservation of the same here in this life to the honour of God, joy and pleasure of my lord the king and us, and the universal wealth, quiet and tranquillity of this whole realm.

Given under our signet at my lord's manor of Hampton Court the 12th day of October,
Jane the Quene.[14]

Preparations now began in earnest for the prince's christening. As the sweating sickness was still circulating, the number of attendees would have to be strictly monitored; both mother and father were not going to take any chances but that didn't mean it couldn't still be magnificent. The date chosen was 15 October. The day began with the prince being carried

Edward VI as a child by Hans Holbein the Younger, c. 1538. Jane provided Henry with his heart's desire, securing her place in his affections and as England's queen but tragically knew her son for only twelve days before she passed away.

from his mother's apartments by the Lady Marquis of Exeter, Gertrude Blount, to the Chapel Royal at Hampton Court Palace where the Archbishop of Canterbury, Thomas Cranmer, performed the baptismal rites. The prince's godparents were his elder half-sister Mary, the dukes of Norfolk and Suffolk and the Archbishop of Canterbury himself; his younger half-sister Elizabeth also had a part to play – she carried the chrisom cloth, helped by Jane's brother Edward.

A description of the christening survives in *Letters and Papers, Foreign and Domestic, Henry VIII*. According to the document, Sirs Francis Bryan, Nicholas Carew, Anthony Browne and John Russell stood around the baptismal font holding aprons and towels whilst the procession entered the chapel. The procession followed a strict hierarchy and went as follows:

First, certain gentlemen two and two bearing torches not lighted until the prince be Christened. Then the children and ministers of the King's chapel, with the dean, 'not singing going outward'. Gentlemen esquires and knights two and two. Chaplains of dignity two and two. Abbots and bishops. The King's councillors. Lords two and two. The comptroller and treasurer of the Household. The ambassadors. The three lords chamberlains and the lord Chamberlain of England in the midst. The lord Cromwell, being lord Privy Seal, and the lord Chancellor. The duke of Norfolk and abp. of Canterbury. A pair of covered basins borne by the earl of Sussex, supported by the lord Montague. A 'taper of virgin wax borne by the earl of Wiltshire in a towel about his neck.' A salt of gold similarly borne by the earl of Essex. 'Then the crysome richly garnished borne by the lady Elizabeth, the King's daughter: the same lady for her tender age was borne by the viscount Beauchamp with the assistance of the lord.' Then the Prince borne under the canopy by the lady marquis of Exeter, assisted by the duke of Suffolk and the marquis her husband. The lady mistress went between the prince and the supporter. The train of the Prince's robe borne by the earl of Arundel and sustained by the lord William Howard.' 'The nurse to go equally with the supporter of the train, and with her the midwife.' The canopy over the Prince borne by Sir Edw. Nevyll, Sir John Wallop, Ric. Long, Thomas Semere, Henry Knyvet, and Mr. Ratclif, of the Privy Chamber. The 'tortayes' of virgin wax borne about the canopy by Sir Humph. Foster, Robt. Turwytt, George Harper, and Ric. Sowthwell. Next after the canopy my lady Mary, being lady godmother, her train borne by lady Kingston. All the other ladies of honour in their degrees.[15]

In a cruel twist of fate, the Earl of Wiltshire was Thomas Boleyn, Anne Boleyn's father. This must have been a day of mixed emotions for him; he had clearly worked himself back into Henry's good graces but he must have spent the christening think about what could have been.

Despite the threat of the sweating sickness, there were an estimated 300 to 400 people in attendance. Following the baptism, the torches were lit and the Garter King of Arms proclaimed the baby's name and titles for the first time: 'God, in his Almighty and infinite grace, grant good life and long to the right high, right excellent, and noble prince Edward, Duke of Cornwall and Earl of Chester, most dear and entirely-beloved son of our most dread and gracious lord Henry VIII.'[16]

The service ended with the singing of the *Te Deum* and the serving of hippocras, bread, spices and wine before Edward was escorted back to his proud and loving parents to receive their blessing; tradition dictated that the king and queen did not attend the christening ceremony as it would take the focus off their child's (and the heir to the throne's) special day. After receiving their blessing Edward was taken to his nursery to sleep; Jane had no such respite. The guests were still in attendance and she needed to be there to receive their congratulations and well wishes and to thank them for their gifts for her son. All the gifts would have been beautiful or valuable or both and included the traditional gold and silver cups and pots (his sister Mary gave him a gold cup); two of his godfathers, the Archbishop and the Duke of Norfolk, both had the same idea and gifted him three bowls and two pots of silver and gilt whilst the third godfather, the Duke of Suffolk, gifted him two flagons and two pots of silver and gilt.

It was after midnight before Jane could retire, but she could do so happy and content with how successful her son's christening had been, how successful her entire pregnancy had been in fact. There had been a longer labour than expected but it was over now and she had her child, her healthy son, which had made all the fears and the pain worth it. Now she could relax, get some rest and regain her strength. Perhaps as she readied herself for bed, she was told by her ladies of the ongoing celebrations in London, that bonfires were lit in her and the prince's honour, and that the church bells were ringing out again in celebration. Perhaps she smiled contentedly as she drifted off to sleep; nothing could ruin her happiness now, she had her husband's love, the court's respect and the people's loyalty and affection; as Henry's wife and queen she was a complete success.

It's tragic that she only had twelve days to enjoy it.

Christening celebrations continued over the following days, the Seymours were riding high in Henry's favour and both Jane's brothers received promotions: Edward was created Earl of Hertford whilst Thomas was knighted and admitted to the Privy Council. Jane is once again a shadowy figure at this time, understandable as she was still in confinement but plans were already being put in place for her churching. The churching ceremony was a thanksgiving service that acknowledged the pains and trouble a new mother had been through and thanked God for her continuing health; it also represented a mother's re-entry to society after childbirth – she was now cleansed and purified. It was not just a religious event but a social one and Jane would have required new clothes for the occasion and so would her ladies.

Now is where things become unclear. I once believed that Jane fell ill soon after Edward's christening, either 16 or 17 October, and endured a period of on/off recovery until 23 October when it was clear something was seriously wrong but now I'm not so sure. Whilst researching this book I have hunted through various articles, books, websites and papers for details of Jane's final days but there is actually very little surviving information. The only concrete evidence of her illness we have is this short message: 'Yesterday afternoon the Queen had "an naturall laxe," by reason of which she seemed to amend till toward night. All night she has been very sick, and rather "appears" than amends. Her confessor has been with her this morning, and is now preparing to minister the Sacrament of Unction.' Signed by Thomas Manners, Earl of Rutland, Robert Aldrich, the Bishop of Carlisle (Jane's confessor) and Jane's physicians, this short note can be found in the *Letters and Papers, Foreign and Domestic Henry VIII Volume 12 Part 2 June–December 1537*, which was originally published by Her Majesty's stationery office, London, in 1891. This letter is dated 24 October but recalls events from the previous day, 23 October.

I can find no mention of Jane's illness before 23 October; whilst it is not impossible that some papers could have been lost over the intervening centuries, we have surviving documents detailing the creation of Edward Seymour as Earl of Hertford and the knighting of Thomas Seymour within the same timeframe that Jane has traditionally been believed to have been ill. Surely something as important as the queen's illness would have survived and been documented more closely? I now believe Jane fell ill suddenly on the 23rd, rapidly declining with some small gaps of respite until she passed away on the 24th.

The confusion may have stemmed from a letter in the British Library, also from Thomas Manners, Earl of Rutland, and Jane's physicians (but not the bishop) which is dated 17 October stating that 'all this night she hath bene very syck and doth rather appare [worsens] then amend'. It goes onto say that Jane's confessor had rushed to her side to 'minister to her grace the sacrament of unction'. This is virtually the same text as the letter we know was written on the 24th.[17]

Illness is unpredictable but it is hard to believe that virtually the same letter was written twice within days of each other; it is more likely that the one from the 17th is misdated. In one way the date becomes irrelevant: whichever is correct, both confirm Jane was now seriously ill and in danger of losing her life. Another letter from Sir John Russell dated 24 October supports this:

> Today the King intended to remove to Esher, and, because the Queen was very sick this night and today, he tarried, but he will be there tomorrow. 'If she amend he will go and if she amend not he told me this day he could not find in his heart to tarry.' She was in great danger yesternight and to day but, if she sleep this night, the physicians hope that she is past danger.[18]

It is hardly surprising Jane became ill: she had endured a long and difficult labour and had then been required to act as hostess to the guests at her son's christening. She had had barely any time to rest; it was an awful lot of strain and activity to put on a newly delivered and exhausted mother. It is easy to believe her health gave way under the strain.

An anxious Henry ordered a solemn intercession of the clergy at St Paul's in order to pray for Jane's recovery. Her ladies rallied round her

Old St Paul's Cathedral in London from *Early Christian Architecture* by Francis Bond (1913). From a copy in the possession of Mr. Crace, Esq., of the earliest known view of London, taken by Van der Wyngarde for Philip II of Spain. A procession of thanksgiving was held here after the birth of Edward but days later a more solemn intercession took place in order to pray for Jane's recovery.

and tried everything they could think of to make her well again. The Chapel Royal at Hampton Court, so recently a place of celebration, was now a site crowded with men and women praying for the queen's health. One witness commented: 'if good prayers can save her, she is not like to die, for never lady was so much plained [popular] with everyman, rich and poor.'[19]

Towards the end Jane's confessor remained in constant attendance, saying prayers and providing comfort as best as he could. It is unclear if Jane was still conscious by this point but hopefully she was, if not all the time, but fleetingly, to receive comfort from her confessor's actions.

In a rare display of sensitivity and foresight, the Duke of Norfolk wrote urgently to Cromwell on the 24th: 'My good lord, I pray you to be here tomorrow early to comfort our good master, for as for our mistress there is no likelihood of her life, the more pity, and I fear she shall not be on lyve at the time ye shall read this.'[20]

Sadly, Norfolk was right, Jane fought a valiant battle right to the end but she was simply too sick to recover. During the night of 24 October 1537, Jane Seymour, third wife and queen of King Henry VIII of England, died in her sleep. She was 29. It is unclear if Henry was with her at the end.

We can't be entirely sure what killed Jane though the traditional belief is puerperal or child bed fever. Puerperal fever is a bacterial infection of the female reproductive tract and symptoms include fever, chills, lower abdominal pain and discharge; causes can be a caesarean, miscarriage, prolonged labour, rupture of the membranes, malnutrition or diabetes. Jane certainly endured a prolonged labour and we know she suffered 'an naturall laxe',[21] which could mean a bleed or bowel movement. The timing also fits, even if we now accept the shorter duration of her illness. Puerperal fever usually occurs after the first twenty-four hours and within the first ten days following delivery. Jane was definitely ill on the 23rd, eleven days after Edward's birth. The term generally used to describe the onset of this infection is 'usually'; infection does not have a schedule and it is possible she was starting to feel ill on the 22nd but either never mentioned it or the symptoms were not noticeable enough at this stage. She would certainly have been at risk of bacteria too – the benefits of clean hands and germs were not understood in Tudors times – today the infection disappears after a course of antibiotics.

Cromwell thought the people serving her bore some responsibility; he wrote to Lord William Howard and Bishop Gardiner: 'They are to announce to Francis that though the Prince is well and "sucketh like a child of his puissance," the queen, by the neglect of those about her who suffered her to take cold and eat such things as her fantasy in sickness called for, is dead.'[22]

Other theories that have been suggested include the possibility that she retained a piece of the placenta that became infected or caused haemorrhaging, sepsis or that she suffered tears in the birth canal that also became infected.

Alison Weir has recently suggested a new possibility: a pulmonary embolism. A pulmonary embolism occurs when a blood vessel in your lungs becomes blocked, usually caused by a blood clot that may have travelled from one of the deep veins in your legs. Lying in bed for long periods of time can increase the chances of an embolism; after Edward's birth Jane was exhausted and required rest in order to recover; barring some slight movement on the day of his christening, she would have been stationery for a long period of time. An embolism can also be caused by a sudden change in your physical condition e.g., surgery or pregnancy and can occur suddenly, which would also fit with the new timeline of Jane's shorter illness.[23]

One common myth that never seems to go away entirely is that Jane underwent a caesarean and died following complications arising from it. This is blatantly untrue. Whilst her contemporaries were aware of the procedure, a caesarean was only ever performed as a last resort, if the mother was already dead or dying. A caesarean on a healthy, pregnant woman in Tudor times would have been an instant death sentence and it wasn't until the nineteenth century that the procedure could be relatively safely carried out. Jane lived for twelve days after Edward's birth, she signed letters announcing her son's birth, greeted guests at his christening and was aware of and took part in plans for her churching, all activities that prove it was impossible for her to have undergone the procedure.

We can trace the origin of the myth to Nicholas Sander, a Catholic recusant in exile, writing during the reign of Elizabeth I. Sander's account is not contemporary and in fact he was only 7 at the time of Edward's birth. He was an opponent of the Reformation who blamed Henry for the destruction of the Roman Catholic Church in England. Sander believed (or professed to) that there was nothing Henry wouldn't do for a son, including sacrificing a wife in childbirth:

> On the 10th day of October [1537], Jane Seymour gave birth to a son, who was named Edward. But the travail of the queen being very difficult, the king was asked which of the two lives was to be spared; he answered, the boy's, because he could easily provide himself with other wives. Jane accordingly died soon after of the pains of childbirth, and was buried at Windsor.[24]

Sander's account became fixed in the minds of Henry's detractors and with each retelling the story became more distorted and embellished, quite drastically in some cases as the description by Nicholas Harpsfield shows. He was writing during the reign of Mary I and was also an opponent of the Reformation:

> Albeit, that mischance also might be accounted among the other great discomforts and misfortunes of his marriage that she should

also die, though for the safeguard of the child, in such a manner as she did; yea, the child to be born, as some say the adders are, by gnawing out the mother's womb.[25]

Habit of Jane Seymour Queen to K. Henry VIII in 1536, c. 1757, artist unknown.

There is a contemporary account alluding to the possibility of a caesarean but it is noted by the unknown author that it was only a rumour they heard. Taken from the *Spanish Chronicle*, a notoriously unreliable document, it states:

In due time, when the Queen was about to be delivered, they sent to London for processions to be made to pray God for a happy result, and after three days illness the most beautiful boy that ever was seen was born. Very great rejoicings were held for his birth; but on the second day it was rumoured that the mother had died, which caused great sorrow. It was said that the mother had to be sacrificed for the child. I do not affirm this to be true, only that it was rumoured.

Later historians included Sander's account in their work but mainly dismiss it as nonsense; the contemporary sources do not back up the story and neither does Jane's good health until the 23rd, eleven days after Edward's birth. The myth did become popular enough to inspire a poem called The *Death of Queen Jane*. There are a few differing versions[26] but the most common one is this:

> *Queen Jeanie, Queen Jeanie, traveld six weeks and more,*
> *Till women and midwives had quite gien her oer:*
> *O if ye were women as women should be,*
> *Ye would send for a doctor, a doctor to me.*
>
> *The doctor was called for and set by her bedside:*
> *'What aileth thee, my ladie, thine eyes seem so red?'*

'O doctor, O doctor, will ye do this for me,
To rip up my two sides and save my babie?'

'Queen Jeanie, Queen Jeanie, that's the thing I'll neer do,
To rip up your two sides to save your babie:'
Queen Jeanie, Queen Jeanie, traveld six weeks and more,
Till women and midwives had quite gien her oer.

'O if you were doctors as doctors should be,
Ye would send for King Henry, King Henry to me:'
King Henry was called for and sat by her bedside,
'What aileth thee, Jeanie? what aileth my bride?'

'King Henry, King Henry, will you do this for me,
To rip up my two sides, and save my babie?'
'Queen Jeanie, Queen Jeanie, that's what I'll never do,
To rip up your two sides to save your babie.'

But with sighing and sobbing she's fallen in a swoon,
Her side it was ript up, and her babie was found;
At this bonnie babie's christning there was meikle joy and mirth,
But bonnie Queen Jeanie lies cold in the earth.

Six and six coaches, and six and six more,
And royal King Henry went mourning before;
O two and two gentlemen carried her away,
But royal King Henry went weeping away.

O black were their stockings, and black were their bands,
And black were the weapons they held in their hands;
O black were their mufflers, and black were their shoes,
And black were the chevrons they drew on their luves.

They mourned in the kitchen, and the mourned in the ha,
But royal King Henry mourned langest of a':
Farewell to fair England, farewell for evermore!
For the fair flower of England will never shine more.[27]

Henry was distraught by Jane's death, so much so that he retreated, like his father before him, into seclusion at Esher to mourn the woman who had given him his son. He commanded the entire court to put on mourning and would himself wear black until early 1538, the only time he ever wore mourning for one of his queens. The Duke of Norfolk and Sir William Paulet were chosen to arrange the queen's funeral. This is involved a bit of research as a queen of England had not died in 'good estate' since Henry's mother, Elizabeth of York, in 1503, over thirty years earlier, Elizabeth's funeral would be used as a blueprint for Jane's.

Sir William Paulet, 1st Marquess of Winchester, by the circle of Hans Eworth, c. 1555. Paulet was the second man tasked with organising Jane's funeral with the Duke of Norfolk.

Shortly after Jane's death her body was prepared for her funeral by the wax chandler 'searing, balming, spicing and trammeling in cloth'. The plumber then 'leaded, soldered and chested; and her entrails were honourably interred in the chapel'.

There was once a sign in the chapel at Hampton Court that displayed this information but it has long since been removed. I contacted Tracy Borman to try to confirm if the story of Jane's heart and internal organs could have been buried there and she kindly spoke to the chaplain who believes this is hearsay with no evidence to support it; however, I asked before I found a direct mention of it in the *Letters and Papers, Foreign and Domestic Henry VIII*. The information can be found in 'A remembrance of the interment of Queen Jane, mother of Edward VI., who died at Hampton Court, 24 Oct., on Wednesday about 12 p.m., in child-bed, 29 Henry VIII'; the document is dated 12 November 1537 and was written by the Heralds' College so perhaps it is true after all.

Jane was dressed in a gold and jewelled robe with a crown set upon her head, and was then moved from her bedchamber to the Chamber of Presence and laid beneath a hearse with twenty-one tapers surrounding her and an altar nearby for mass to be sung.[28] Her ladies dressed in their

The Chapel Royal in Hampton Court Palace, c. 1839. Jane's son Edward was christened here with great pomp and celebration but a more sombre atmosphere would prevail when Jane laid in state in the same chapel just over a week later.

mourning clothes kept a vigil over her night and day. On All Saints Day Jane was moved to the chapel through the same halls that were so recently richly decorated in celebration and were now covered in the black cloth of mourning. In the chapel another hearse waited to receive her, this one decorated with banner rolls displaying her, Henry's and Edward's descent.

The king's officers and servants arrived and stood double rank with unlit torches whilst Jane's loyal confessor, the Bishop of Carlisle, with the Bishop of Chichester, the dean and subdean performed the obsequies. As the torches were lit the Lancaster herald called out to the mourners, 'Of your charity pray for the soul of the queen.' Her stepdaughter Mary was her chief mourner but was so overcome with emotion on this day she felt unable to attend the services and her place was taken briefly by the Marquis of Exeter. Mary had recovered enough by the following day to perform her duties for the rest of the procession.[29]

Jane's loss had not just devastated her husband but Mary too and she pushed herself hard to ensure her friend and stepmother received exactly what was due to her. Mary took control of Jane's household, distributing the funeral dole to each servant and was quite generous with the amounts given; she also paid for masses to be said for Jane's soul.[30]

For the next eleven days the chapel was filled with masses, prayers and offerings for the late queen and watch was kept over her night and day. In London the Lord Mayor ordered 1,200 masses to be sung 'for the Soul of our most gracious Queen', followed by a great ceremony to honour her:

> there was a knyll [knell] rongen in everie parishe churche in London, from 12 of the clocke as no one tyll six of the clocke at night with all the bells ringing in every parishe churche solemne peales from 3 of the clocke tyll the knylls ceased; and also a solemne dirige songen in everye parishe churche in London, and in everie churche of freeres [friars], monkes, and chanons, about London; and the morrow after a solemne masse of requiem in all the sayde churches with all the bells ringing from 9 of the clocke in the morning tyll no one.[31]

On 12 November Jane left Hampton Court for the last time and began her final journey to Windsor Castle. Her casket was carried on a chariot drawn by six horses, on top of which lay an effigy showing her as she was in life. Richly dressed in robes of state and wearing gold shoes and embroidered stockings, the effigy held a sceptre in its right hand and wore rings and a crown, displaying to the world that she had died an honoured queen.[32] Mary riding a horse covered in black velvet was noticeably prominent in the procession that included Cromwell and Cranmer, almost the entire nobility, ambassadors, knights, the clergy,

Funeral of Elizabeth I of England, by an unknown artist, c. 1603. The detail in this image gives us an idea what Jane's funeral procession looked like.

minstrels and trumpet players, the latter two proclaiming the queen's last journey to the world. Two almoners distributed alms to the surrounding crowd and 200 poor men carrying torches and wearing Jane's badge of the phoenix also walked in the procession. The entire cavalcade was greeted by silent crowds who bowed their heads in respect as Jane's casket passed.[33]

It is traditionally believed that twenty-nine ladies walked in procession behind Jane's casket, which seems like an odd number until you learn that each lady may have represented a year of her life. I contacted Alison Weir to see if she could point me in the right direction of the source of this tradition as I first came across it in her book *The Six Wives of Henry VIII* but, unfortunately, she hasn't been able to lay her hands on her notes. However, something similar occurred at Elizabeth of York's funeral in 1503. The Lady Mayoress of London

Elizabeth of York by an unknown artist, c. 1470–98. Elizabeth and Jane would appear to share many characteristics and it may be that Jane reminded Henry of his much-loved mother and couldn't help making the comparison that both of them were perfect queens for their husbands. Elizabeth's funeral was used as a precedent on how to conduct Jane's with the proper dignity and respect due to a Queen of England as a queen had not died in 'good estate' since Elizabeth herself in 1503.

arranged for thirty-seven virgins wearing white linen and wreaths on their heads in the Tudor colours (green and white) to hold burning tapers and stand in Cheapside to honour the queen as her casket passed by. Thirty-seven is another unusual number but it is also Elizabeth's age when she died. We know Elizabeth's funeral was used as a model for Jane's so it's certainly possible the same happened in 1537.[34 & 35]

At Windsor the procession was greeted by the Mayor of London and his brethren, each carrying a lit torch. They escorted Jane's body to the outer gate where they were greeted by the Dean of Windsor and the entire college; she was then reverently carried beneath a canopy into St George's Chapel through the west door, where the Archbishop of Canterbury, with numerous bishops and abbots waited to receive her. The casket was placed in a prominent position under another hearse whilst the dirige and lessons were read by the bishops and abbots. Afterwards the majority of the company retired for the night, leaving a small group to keep a solemn watch for the final time.

On the morning of the 13th, the mourners gathered for the service of interment. It began with the offering of 'palles'. A palle (or pall) is an expensive cloth that covers a casket at a funeral; there is no set amount that can be given but at Jane's funeral the Ladies Bray, Dawbeney, Morley and Cobham offered one, Ladies Margaret Howard and Marg Grey two and the Countesses of Southampton, Bath, Sussex, Rutland

Windsor Castle. Jane rests in St George's Chapel at Windsor; she had retreated there during her pregnancy. (*Author's Collection*)

St George's Chapel at Windsor Castle. Jane was laid to rest here after a magnificent ceremony on 13 November 1537. Jane was the only one of Henry's wives to be buried as queen and ten years later he would order his own internment beside her. (*Author's Collection*)

and Derby three. Lady Frances Brandon (daughter of Henry's younger sister) gave four whilst Mary gave seven. Mary and the other mourners then retired to the castle where they were 'sumptuously provided for' and Jane was quietly laid to rest in a vault in the Quire of St George's Chapel. Everything was complete by 12 o'clock.[36]

Chapter 9

After Jane

As custom dictated, Henry did not attend his wife's funeral; instead, he remained in seclusion at Esher, conducting only essential business through a small group of trusted advisors. Henry's grief was genuine, even admitting it to his rival Francis I:

> I have so cordially received the congratulations, which, by this bearer and by your letters, you have made me for the son which it has pleased God to give me, that I desire nothing more than an occasion by the success of your good desires to make the like. Notwithstanding, Divine Providence has mingled my joy with the bitterness of the death of her who brought me this happiness.[1]

He received messages of condolences from various sources, even from the Doge of Venice. Closer to home Bishop Tunstall wrote to the king and pointed out various pieces of scripture for his consolation but admitted to Cromwell he did not want to press the matter as it was still too soon.

It was not just Henry who was mourning; the people of England regarded Jane's death as a tragic loss and were sorry for it. Thomas Knyght wrote to Cromwell on 12 November, commenting how good she must have been as she left such regret in the minds of all.[2] Whilst others were saddened, her son had been left motherless and she hadn't had the chance to have more children. One of the few to have access to Henry at this time, Norfolk, exhorted him to accept God's pleasure in taking the queen and recomfort himself with the treasure sent to him and this realm.[3] Both Henry and England would do this and there was often a combination of grief at Jane's death but joy at her son's birth.

Jane's affairs were settled during this time; her 'jointure', property she held as Queen of England, was returned to her husband whilst a list was made of her jewels and outstanding debts. An entry in the Book of the Queen's Jewels written shortly after her death shows that Jane was quite a generous mistress. As queen she had an enormous collection of jewellery available to her but she made presents of it too. The book shows she gave various gifts of beads, brooches, jewels, borders, girdles, bracelets, pomanders and tablets to her ladies and stepdaughters. She also gave gifts to male members of the court and her household too, as a Mr Worsley had charge of buttons of gold and borders at her death whilst there are thirteen names listed as receiving a brooch from her including a Mr Thomas Seamowre, which could be Jane's own brother.[4]

Jane was a good sister to another of her brothers too; in a list of debts owed to her on her death is one from a Ric Warren of Bekensfeld Bucks. Jane paid his debt to Henry Seymour but was still waiting to be paid back herself when she died. Jane appointed Henry her receiver for her properties of Berkehamstede and King's Langley and also appointed him her bailiff and steward at a number of other properties, showing the trust and affection she held for him. Her other brother, Edward, actually owed her money in rent for Londonwyke, a property once part of the monastery of Stanley.[5]

As Jane's affairs looked to be wrapped up, Henry's council started looking for his next wife. In the same letter Cromwell wrote to Lord William Howard and Bishop Gardiner, detailing Jane's death; he wrote:

> The King, though he takes this chance reasonably, is little disposed to marry again, but some of his Council have thought it meet for us to urge him to it for the sake of his realm, and he has 'framed his mind, both to be indifferent to the thing and to the election of any person from any part that with deliberation shall be thought meet.' Two persons in France might be thought on, viz., the French king's daughter (said to be not the meetest) and Madame de Longueville, of whose qualities you are to inquire, and also on what terms the King of Scots stands with either of them. Lord William must not return without ascertaining this, but the inquiry must be kept secret.[6]

Whilst Henry was grief stricken at Jane's death, he knew the realities of the situation; he had a son but he needed 'a spare'. He himself had only come to the throne because his elder brother had died, but it is worth noting that Henry had to be persuaded to start the search for a fourth wife.

Henry would be married three more times, but he would never produce any more children. The gap between his third and fourth marriages was the longest time Henry was ever unwed and whilst grief would be one of the reasons for this delay, it was also difficult to find a woman who wanted to marry him. In two years, Henry had lost three queens and very few women wanted to accept such a dangerous position. Henry was also no longer the physically attractive suitor he supposed himself to be. One candidate, Christina of Denmark, Duchess of Milan, described as 'not so pure white as the late queen'[7] but not easily paralleled in beauty and birth, famously said that if she 'had two heads, one should be at the disposal of the King of England',[8] a pointed reference to the fate of Anne Boleyn. Mary of Guise, upon hearing a comment Henry had said about needing a big wife, responded, 'I may be a big woman, but I have a very little neck.'[9]

Christina of Denmark, Duchess of Milan, by Hans Holbein the Younger, c. 1538. A possible bride after Jane's death, she was less than enthusiastic saying that if she 'had two heads, one should be at the disposal of the King of England'.

In 1540, three years after Jane's death, Henry would choose Anne of Cleves as his fourth queen after seeing a portrait Hans Holbein had produced of her. The marriage lasted just six months. Whilst he may not have referred to her as a 'Flanders Mare', he certainly didn't like Anne once he met her, complaining that she was not as good looking as people had described, however his rejection may have come about following her unintentional embarrassment of him.

Mary of Guise attributed to Corneille de Lyon, c. 1537. Another prospective bride of Henry after Jane's death, she famously commented after hearing Henrys comments about her that 'I may be a big woman, but I have a very little neck',

Anne of Cleves, Henry VIII's fourth wife, by Hans Holbein the Younger, c. 1539. Jane's immediate successor, she was Queen of England for just six months after Henry claimed he could not consummate their marriage.

Henry had waited impatiently for Anne's arrival and once he heard she had landed in England, rode to meet her but he went in disguise as part of a courtly love tradition, the idea being Anne would immediately recognise her intended and the couple would fall in love on sight.

However, Anne hadn't received the same education as some of his earlier and later wives. Her education appears to have been strictly limited to reading and writing German and sewing. She had no idea of the concept of courtly love and when approached by a strange man trying to kiss her, this virtuous woman rightly turned away, and from this moment Henry tried his best to get out of the marriage but he couldn't afford to offend Anne's brother, William, Duke of Jülich-Cleves-Berg, as Charles V and Francis I were currently enjoying a period of friendship that left England isolated. If he rejected his sister, he would push William into the arms of his two rivals.

With a new wife came her ladies and once again Henry fell in love, this time, with a cousin of his second wife Catherine Howard. His love for her propelled him into action and an investigation was quickly launched into the validity of Henry and Anne's marriage. Whilst his first marriage had taken years to undo, the one to Anne of Cleves took just over two weeks, and it was annulled on the grounds of a previous pre-contract and non-consummation. Anne did not fight the annulment and in return she was given a generous settlement by her grateful ex-husband, awarded properties, a pension and from then on regarded as the king's beloved sister; she also retained precedence over other ladies at court apart from the queen and the king's daughters.

Portrait of an unknown lady possibly Catherine Howard, Henry VIII's fifth wife, by Hans Holbein the Younger, c. 1540. Catherine was the second wife to be executed on Henry's orders after rumours of her past and current suspicious behaviour became common knowledge. She was a cousin of Anne Boleyn and half-second cousin to Jane.

Just over two weeks later Henry married Catherine Howard on the same day of his once-right-hand man's execution. Cromwell had fallen out of favour as he had championed the Cleves marriage and whilst officially found guilty of heresy and treason, it was an open secret what had actually brought him down. Henry was besotted with Catherine; one witness wrote that he caressed her more than he did the others and constantly showered her with gifts. Catherine provided Henry with a new lease of life as he started rising early and exercising more, well aware of the significant age gap between them.

However not everything was as it seemed. Catherine had been a poorer relation in the Howard family and had been brought up in the Dowager Duchess of Norfolk's household. The dowager was a less-than-vigilant guardian and many of her wards ran riot behind her back. The older girls often stole food and drink from the kitchens and held gatherings in their sleeping chambers, and worse – they invited men. Catherine was easily sucked into the fun and may not have realised the danger she was in when she became the object of two men's desire. The first man was her music teacher, Henry Manox; the couple do not appear to have slept together according to their later accounts – they engaged in 'sexual contact' and flirting but that was as far as it went. The second man was

Francis Dereham, a secretary to the dowager, and this relationship was consummated; witnesses later remembered them calling each other husband and wife and Dereham left money with Catherine whilst he travelled abroad, clearly trusting her and perhaps believing they were married or would be soon.

To make matters worse, whilst on Progress as queen, she was observed acting suspiciously and indulged in secret meetings with Thomas Culpepper, a favourite of Henry's. The only lady she allowed to serve her at these meetings was Lady Jane Rochford, the widow of George Boleyn. Rumours of her strange behaviour reached the Archbishop of Canterbury who quietly started investigating the young queen but it was information from John Lassells, whose sister had once served in the dowager's household, that destroyed the fairytale. Henry initially refused to believe the accusations but when confronted with Manox's, Dereham's and later Catherine's confessions he was forced to accept the horrible truth. At first it looked like Catherine would merely be dismissed from court in disgrace; there was a possible case for bigamy if it could be proved she and Dereham were in fact married but when Culpepper's name was brought up, events took a deadly turn. Neither ever confessed to sleeping together and Catherine would claim he actually pestered her with Lady Rochford's encouragement, but their fates were sealed when Culpepper confessed that 'he intended and meant to do ill with the Queen and in likewise the queen so minded to do with him'.[10] Dereham and Culpepper were executed on 10 December 1541. Two months later Catherine Howard and Lady Jane Rochford were beheaded at the Tower of London.

Despite the shock and pain caused by his fifth marriage, Henry would marry for the sixth and final time on 12 July 1543, to Catherine Parr, the widow of Lord Latimer. Catherine, like Jane, promoted reconciliation especially amongst her new family, and she would become close to each of Henry's very different children and even helped convince Henry to restore his daughters to the line of succession though he would not legitimise them. She was directly involved in the education of Elizabeth and Edward, personally choosing their tutors but did not forget her own family, making her sister and stepdaughter her ladies in waiting.

In April 1544, Catherine anonymously published a book titled *Psalms or Prayers taken out of Holy Scriptures*; the work was a translation of an earlier Latin work by Bishop John Fisher. The psalms and prayers included were focused on defeating enemies and praying for the king, as in July Henry would travel to France on his last campaign, leaving Catherine as regent in his place. Catherine signed five proclamations, handled provisions, finances and musters for Henry's army and even kept in constant correspondence with her deputy in the North who was keeping an eye on the unstable situation in Scotland.

CATHARINA REGINA VXOR HENRICI VIII

After the success of her first book Catherine, published her second, *Prayers or Meditations*, in June 1545, this time with her name on it. She was the first Englishwoman to have a book published under her own name.[11] A year later she found herself nearing disgrace and possible death when she was suspected of being a Protestant. Catherine was a supporter of religious reform and after Henry's death would embrace Protestantism wholeheartedly but at

Catherine Parr, Henry VIII's sixth wife; copy of a lost portrait by Hans Eworth from 1548 by the English school. Catherine would help bring Henry's family together and was loved and respected by each of his three very different children; to Edward she became the mother he had never had. After Henry's death she married Thomas Seymour and therefore became Jane's sister in-law as well as her successor as queen.

this time her enemies, notably the anti-Protestant Bishop of Winchester, and Lord Wriothesley, the Lord Chancellor, tried to move against her. When Catherine was observed to be contradicting an annoyed Henry in religious matters the two men leapt at the chance and persuaded an angry Henry to order her arrest and interrogation. Whether through luck or design, Catherine saw the warrant and after a near breakdown, managed to compose herself and convinced her husband that she had only disagreed with his opinions in order to better educate herself and take Henry's mind off his bad legs which were now a constant source of agony to him. Henry was convinced by her explanation and the couple were reconciled but he forgot (or deliberately forgot) to inform Gardiner and Wriothesley of their reconciliation, resulting in an awkward and frightening confrontation with an armed guard whilst Catherine and Henry walked in the gardens together.

The rest of their married life was as peaceful as could be and when Henry died, he left Catherine a rich widow with orders that she was to be treated as queen as if he still lived; despite her proven capabilities as regent, she was not appointed or even included in the minority council. With no role in government Catherine instead picked up where she left off; before she had attracted the eye of the king, she had been romantically involved with Thomas Seymour, Jane's brother, but had had to give him up at the first sign of Henry's interest. Six months after Henry's death, the two were discreetly married, making Henry's third wife posthumously the sister-in-law of his sixth. Catherine would not get to enjoy her happiness for long; her younger stepdaughter Elizabeth had come to live with her after her father's death and her husband started to show an inappropriate interest in her. Meanwhile Catherine had fallen pregnant and whilst aware of some of Thomas's behaviour, she was shocked to discover Thomas in a clinch with Elizabeth. An upset Catherine immediately sent a guilt-ridden Elizabeth away and covered up the potential scandal. The

Stained-glass window in the Great Hall at Hampton Court Palace showing Henry VIII surrounded by the coats of arms of his wives. (*Author's Collection*)

two would correspond by letter and reconcile before Catherine's death. On 30 August Catherine gave birth to her and Thomas's only child, a daughter they called Mary after her elder stepdaughter. Like Jane before her, Catherine fell ill, probably with childbed fever and died five days later, on 5 September 1548. Catherine was married to England's most married king but she herself remains England's most married queen, marrying a total of four times.

Henry died on 28 January 1547. At his funeral only the badges and arms of two of his wives were carried in the funeral procession: Jane Seymour's and Catherine Parr's; as far as Henry was

Edward VI of England, c. 1546, attributed to William Scrots. Jane's son became king at the age of 9 and his reign saw the beginning of Protestantism in England but he would never reach his majority, dying aged 15 in 1553.

concerned, they were his only true wives.[12] In his last will and testament, which was contested then and now, he asked to be laid to rest beside the woman he had continued to respect and honour, to include in family portraits and the mother of his son, at Windsor Castle:

> directs that it shall be laid in the choir of his college of Windesour, midway between the stalls and the high altar, in a tomb now almost finished in which he will also have the bones of his wife, Queen Jane. And there an altar shall be furnished for the saying of daily masses while the world shall endure.[13]

Their son became Edward VI on his father's death but he was only 9 years old and so a regency council was established to rule on his behalf until he was 18. This part of the will was not entirely honoured as Edward Seymour, who became Duke of Somerset after Henry's death, was also created Lord Protector of England and, whilst a council had

Closeup of the roundels on the ceiling of the Great Watching Chamber at Hampton Court Palace; in the centre is Jane's badge of a phoenix rising from a castle. (*Author's Collection*)

been created, Seymour started to rule as if he was king himself, angering his fellow councillors with his arrogance. He soon faced opposition over his policies, the war in Scotland and general social unrest. During this time, he and Thomas fell out. Thomas believed that as they were both uncles of the king, they should have equal responsibilities but Somerset had taken control of both the country and the king's person. Thomas had been promoted as 1st Baron Seymour of Sudeley and Lord High Admiral but his jealousy and anger continued to fester, leading him into plots to unseat his brother and take control of his nephew. He married Henry's last queen, Catherine Parr, and, as mentioned, attempted to seduce her younger stepdaughter Elizabeth whilst they lived together. After Catherine died Thomas became even more frantic in his efforts to secure power and overthrow his brother, even attempting to influence the king but Edward, wise for such a young age, seemed to know he was up to something and maintained a neutral stance throughout.

Events during the night of 16 January 1549 would prove to be Thomas's downfall; whilst the exact intentions and motives are unclear, Thomas was found outside his nephew's bedchamber at Hampton Court and upon disturbing the king's pet dog, he shot and killed it to stop it barking. Thomas claimed he was checking his nephew's security but his actions were interpreted in the worst possible light and he was arrested and sent to the Tower the next day. After being accused of thirty-three counts of treason and convicted, he was condemned to death and executed on 20 March 1549.

The Duke of Somerset had tried to save his brother, calling a council meeting so Thomas could explain his actions but the events of 16 January took things out of his control. Somerset would not outlive his brother by very long. By October 1549 his own position was in jeopardy and, doing what many suspected Thomas of trying to do, took possession of his nephew and retreated with him to the safety of Windsor Castle where he issued a proclamation asking for assistance. Edward VI was not happy at this turn of events saying, 'Methinks I am in prison.' On 11 October Somerset was arrested by the council, the king was freed and brought to Richmond where he summarised the charges against Somerset: 'Ambition, vainglory, entering into rash wars in mine youth, negligent looking on Newhaven, enriching himself of my treasure, following his own opinion, and doing all by his own authority, etc.'[14]

Somerset would be released and readmitted to the council but his time as protector was over; instead, John Dudley, Earl of Warwick, emerged as the new leader though he never called himself Lord Protector, perhaps recognising the title itself was now tainted. Somerset would be arrested again in October 1551 on what many believed was an exaggerated charge of treason. He was later convicted and executed for felony in January 1552 for plotting to overthrow Dudley's regime. Somerset was laid to rest in the Chapel of St Peter Ad Vincula at the Tower of London, the same chapel where his brother was buried after his execution back in 1549.

The young king appeared to take all of this in his stride, showing very little emotion at the deaths of two of his uncles. All he wrote of Somerset's death was: 'the duke of Somerset had his head cut off upon Tower Hill between eight and nine o'clock in the morning.' This sentence can be found in a chronicle Edward kept. The chronicle is an interesting document but it doesn't reveal Edward's thoughts and emotions; it is more a record of his own reign in his own hand, focusing on notable events and military manoeuvres. However, there is a surviving source showing Edward expressing guilt and sorrow for his uncles' and even for his mother's death. Written by Antonio de Guaras, a Spanish merchant and later ambassador, he wrote:

albeit the king gave no token of any ill discomposed passions, as taking it not agreeable to Majesty openly to declare himself … yet upon speech of him he would often sigh and let fall tears. Sometimes holding opinion that his uncle had done nothing; or if he had it was very small and proceeded from his wife rather than himself, and where then, said he, was the good nature of a Nephew, where was the clemency of a Prince? Ah, how unfortunate have I been to those of my blood. My mother I slew at my birth and since have made away two of her brothers.[15]

Edward VI's reign was notable for its economic problems and social unrest that erupted into riot and rebellion but his greatest achievement was the transformation of the Church of England into a noticeably Protestant body. Edward was a firm Protestant and greatly interested in religious matters and debate. He encouraged reformers and supported the mandatory conduction of services in English; the mass and clerical celibacy were also abolished. Edward appeared to have the makings of a firm and intelligent king but in January 1553, he fell ill with a cough and fever that he struggled to recover from. At first there were hopes for his recovery and he did enjoy periods of remission but would sicken again with worse symptoms, including coughing up blood and yellow and black matter. It was soon clear that Edward was terminally ill; he quickly wasted away to nothing, barely leaving him with the energy to cough to clear his airway; his legs swelled up and in his final days he was confined to his bed. Edward VI died on 6 July 1553, aged 15; he never reached his majority. As with most sudden royal deaths, rumours of poison spread but when his body was opened his lungs were found to be diseased, leading most historians to believe consumption or tuberculosis as it is now known as the cause of his death. The Tudor males seemed to be susceptible to consumption as both Prince Arthur and Henry Fitzroy were believed to have died of a similar wasting disease.

Edward was laid to rest in his grandfather's chapel at Westminster Abbey where his grave remained unmarked until 1966 when Christ's Hospital School paid for an inscribed stone to commemorate their founder. The inscription reads: 'In memory of King Edward VI buried in this chapel. This stone was placed here by Christ's Hospital in thanksgiving for their founder, 7 October 1966.'[16]

The son for whom Henry VIII had torn England apart and the son for whom Jane had given her life died young and England faced the prospect of its first queen regnant.

To try and prevent his Catholic half-sister Mary from inheriting his throne and undoing his reforms, Edward nominated their cousin, Lady Jane Grey, a committed Protestant, to inherit after him but she was not widely supported and is now known as the 'Nine Days' Queen' after her deposition by Mary and her supporters. Jane and her husband were tried for their part in the usurpation, found guilty and sentenced to death but it was widely believed that Mary would spare them, knowing that their actions were not their own.

Lady Jane Grey by Willem van de Passe, c. 1620. Edward attempted to leave his throne to Jane as she was a committed Protestant like himself and he knew she would carry on his work for the Church of England.

Mary would reign for five years and as Edward suspected she did undo his reforms, returning England to the Church of Rome briefly. She would marry Phillip II of Spain and it was these negotiations that triggered a rebellion in favour of deposing Mary and replacing her with sister Elizabeth. Mary regained control but was forced to execute her young cousin to prevent her being used as a figurehead. Lady Jane Grey and her husband, Lord Guildford Dudley, were executed on 12 February 1554. Elizabeth was arrested and interrogated but there was no concrete evidence that she had been involved so she was released and placed under house arrest. Mary tried to produce an heir but suffered two phantom pregnancies that left her distraught; it's possible the symptoms she thought were of pregnancy were actually of the disease that killed her which is believed to have been cancer. She died on 17 November 1558, aged 42.

Elizabeth took the throne after her sister and, unlike her siblings, her reign would be long, lasting forty-five years and providing stability for a much-shaken nation. Elizabeth reinstated many of her brother's reforms but always tried to tread a middle way through the religious differences in England. She was cautious in foreign affairs and reluctant to embark on military campaigns. She faced down several conspiracies thanks to her spy network and saw off the Spanish Armada sent by her former brother-in-law. Elizabeth never married or produced an heir. The Tudor dynasty died with her in 1603; today she is known as the Virgin Queen.

Three of Jane's siblings would live to see Elizabeth reign but their mother would not. Margery Seymour passed away during her grandson's reign, in October 1550. Her eldest son petitioned the council for a state funeral for the king's grandmother but it was a sign of how far he had fallen when his request was denied.[17] Elizabeth Seymour died on 19 March 1568. Her marriage to Gregory had produced five children but, like her first husband, he would predecease her. At the time of her death she was married to her third husband, John Paulet, 2nd Marquess of Winchester. Dorothy died on 4 January 1574, predeceasing her second husband, and Henry died on 5 April 1578; it is not known when his wife died.

For a time, above Jane's grave was the inscription:

Here lieth a Phoenix, by whose death,
Another phoenix life gave breath:
It is to be lamented much
The world at once ne'er knew two such

The inscription has long since been lost and today a marble slab marks Jane's resting place.[18] The slab is beautiful in its simplicity but it was not at all what Henry had in mind. Early in his reign he had made plans for a joint tomb for himself and his first wife and from what documentation survives, it was to be magnificent and we can assume he had no less planned for himself and Jane.

The tomb he had intended to share with Catherine was to include a marble sarcophagus with 'ten soaring marble pillars on top of which would be a figure an apostle and in the centre a life-sized figure of the King mounted on a horse'. It was to be 25 per cent bigger than his parents' monument and, if you are lucky enough to visit Westminster Abbey, you can get an idea of the size Henry had in mind.[19] For decoration there was to be gold-covered brass figures of saints, angels, semi-precious oriental stones and nine-foot candlesticks. What some don't know is that parts of the tomb were actually recycled. The marble sarcophagus and the angels were originally meant for Cardinal Wolsey's tomb but when he fell from favour, Henry kept these parts for his own tomb.[20]

Work on the monument was erratic, possibly as Henry, like his daughter Elizabeth, was not fond of facing his mortality. The monument was an expensive project the country could ill afford. Henry later wanted a 'recumbent statue of his most entirely beloved wife Queen Jane'[21] to be built, including four life-size images of the couple. Henry and Jane were only supposed to rest in the vault temporarily and then be moved once the tomb was completed. By the time of Henry's death, the project had been taken over by an artist named Benedetto but work was still incomplete.

Each of Henry's children tried to complete the tomb but Edward's and Mary's reigns were short and may account for the lack of progress. Elizabeth had her treasurer compile a report to see what still remained to be done; she gathered all the separate parts that had been produced and stored them in a 'tomb house' at Windsor but ultimately, due to lack of interest, time or funds, Elizabeth was never able to complete the tomb either.

Admiral Horatio Nelson's tomb in the Crypt of St Paul's by Thomas Hosmer Shepherd, c. 1830. He is interred in a sarcophagus originally meant for Cardinal Thomas Wolsey and later repurposed by Henry VIII after Wolseys' fall from favour. Henry's tomb was never completed so the sarcophagus was repurposed again for Admiral Nelson.

Henry and Jane were left to rest in peace until 1649 when their vault was opened and they were joined by another famous king, the ill-fated Charles I. The death of Charles I, in a roundabout way, finalised the decision regarding Henry's tomb. The commonwealth government that replaced the monarchy was desperately short of funds, so they sold off the parts that had been built and some still survive to this day: four of the candlesticks can be found in Belgium in the St Bavo Cathedral,[22] whilst closer to home the sarcophagus was recycled again and today forms part of the tomb of Admiral Lord Nelson in St Paul's Cathedral, London.[23] Finally, four angels now known as the 'Wolsey Angels' are in the Victoria and Albert Museum. The angels had been mounted on top of gate posts at Harrowden Hall in Northamptonshire but two had later been sold at auction where they were attributed to Benedetto; the other two remained at Harrowden Hall and once it was confirmed all four were in fact part of the tomb, the Victoria and Albert Museum purchased them for £5 million.[24]

Years later it would be opened once more in order to inter an infant child of Queen Anne; the child would be the last interment in the vault. After some time, and fading human memory, the vault was lost and it was not rediscovered until 1813 – by accident. George III had ordered the construction of a new royal mausoleum in St George's Chapel and it was during construction that Jane and Henry's vault was rediscovered. Supervised by the Prince Regent (later George IV), the vault was opened for the first time in over 100 years. The coffin of Charles I lies on the far-left side of the vault with the tiny coffin of Queen Anne's child resting on top, Henry's coffin is in the middle and Jane's rests on the far right. Whilst Jane's, Charles's and the child's coffins were intact, Henry's was badly damaged.

There are a few ways this could have happened: as Henry's body decomposed, gases would have been produced and they could have 'blown' open the coffin. It appears it wasn't structurally sound to begin with as a story has come down to us that when it rested at Syon Abbey on its journey to Windsor Castle in 1547, it apparently broke apart and fluids were seen to leak on the floor and were licked up by a dog,[25] fulfilling a prophecy made when Henry was trying to divorce his first wife.[26] Another possibility is that that the damage occurred when the vault was opened to inter Charles. Henry's coffin could have been damaged by the opening of the tomb or the lowering of Charles's coffin into the vault. Another alternative is that the trestle it rested on collapsed or Henry's coffin was dropped whilst he was being interred. The damage was bad enough that the coffin was now open and the Prince Regent was able to see Henry's skeleton and clinging to the jaw of the skull were the traces of a beard.[27]

In a fit of ghoulish curiosity Charles I's coffin was opened and some 'relics' were taken, but luckily Jane was left undisturbed – the Prince Regent decided that mere curiosity was not enough to disturb her remains. The vault was resealed and the Prince Regent commanded that a marble slab should mark the resting place of these famous figures; this was not done until his brother William IV's reign in 1837. The marble plaque reads:

In a vault
beneath this marble slab
are deposited the remains
of
Jane Seymour Queen of King Henry VIII
1537
King Henry VIII
1547
King Charles I
1648
and
an infant child of Queen Anne.

This memorial was placed here by command of King William IV.
1837

Modern research suggests that the memorial is not in the right place and actually lies to the west of the vault. The vault was opened for the final time in 1888 on the orders of the Prince of Wales, the future King Edward VII. Bertie as he was known to his family and friends wanted to reinter the relics taken from Charles I's coffin in 1813. It was during this opening that Alfred Young Nutt, the Surveyor of the Fabric to the College of St George, made a sketch showing the resting place of each individual, which is probably the only visual we will ever have of the inside of Jane and Henry's tomb.[28]

As Elizabeth Jane Timms noted in her article about Jane's grave in 2019, the marble slab records that Henry lays with his Queen, JANE: there is no mention of the fact that she was his third queen. It could almost be read as she was his only wife and queen (if you didn't know any better); perhaps Henry would have approved of this at least.[29]

Water colour of the inside of the vault under the Quire of St George's Chapel, Windsor Castle. Charles I's coffin is on the left with the infant child of Queen Anne resting on top, Henry VIII's is in the centre and Jane Seymour's is on the right; today the vault is marked by a marble slab in the floor. Jane's coffin has never been disturbed. Water colour by Alfred Young Nutt, Surveyor to the Dean and Canons of St George's Chapel, Windsor Castle, c. 1888.

The marble slab that marks Jane's and Henry's resting place today. Whilst quite elegant in its simplicity, it's not at all what Henry had in mind. (© St George's Chapel, reproduced with kind permission and licence)

In March 2022, I was fortunate enough to travel to London and managed to cram in all three of my bucket-list destinations: the Tower of London, Hampton Court Palace and Windsor Castle. Hampton Court was the place I was most excited to visit and it didn't disappoint. The Great Hall is magnificent with its large stained-glass windows depicting the descent of each of Henry's wives; the windows are not Tudor survivors – they were installed during the reign of Queen Victoria – but are gorgeous to see, especially when the sun hits them. There is a subtle Tudor survivor in the hall; if you know where to look you will find a missed entwined H&A that should have been destroyed after Anne's execution. I wonder if Jane saw it and, if so, what did she feel?

Signs and symbols of Jane can still be found in the Great Watching Chamber with its unique roundel ceiling. The roundels depict Henry VIII's coat of arms, the Tudor rose, the French fleur-de-lis and Jane's badge as queen. The coat of arms of Henry and Jane can be found outside the chapel where her son was christened and where she lay in state after her death. The ceiling of the chapel is beautifully decorated; photos do not

One of the original Tudor rose roundels on display in the Great Watching Chamber at Hampton Court Palace. (*Author's Collection*)

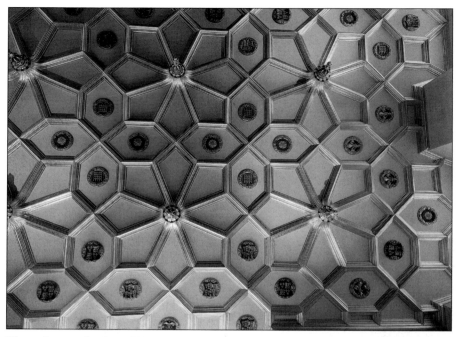

The ceiling in the Great Watching Chamber at Hampton Court Palace. The roundels all make reference to Henry VIII and Jane Seymour's marriage; the designs include Jane's phoenix badge, the Tudor rose, the French fleur-de-lis and Henry VIII's coat of arms. Some of the roundels are more modern replicas but one or two are still the originals. (*Author's Collection*)

do it justice. Next to the chapel is a recreated Tudor garden filled with beautifully coloured Tudor heraldic beasts, one of which is Jane's spotted panther. These beasts are based on similar ones found at the entrance to the palace but these are made of stone and unpainted. These beasts were restored at the beginning of the twentieth century but were derived from originals created in 1536/7 to celebrate Henry and Jane's marriage; each holds a shield displaying a coat of arms or heraldic badge.

However, it was St George's Chapel at Windsor Castle that ended up having the biggest impact on me. As I entered the Quire, I immediately spotted the marble plaque in the floor. The area was quite full so I stayed back until some of the visitors had left. I remember being surprised at its size; I think because I'd become used to reading about Henry's grand designs for the tomb, in my mind the plaque had become small. I had wanted to visit and pay my respects to the woman who has fascinated me for so long and I couldn't believe I was finally doing so; I was both excited and nervous. When things quietened down, I approached and

The king's crowned lion displaying the impaled arms of Henry VIII and Jane Seymour. (*Author's Collection*)

knelt down to take a closer look. The plaque is clean and well maintained despite the number of visitors that step on it. I found myself thinking how sad it was that Jane died when she did; she had given Henry a son and heir, she was safe and secure, Henry would never set aside the mother of his son. Ignoring the politics, she was also a first-time mother, and as she held her beautiful baby boy in her arms she must have thought of the future. Would Edward grow strong? Would he have brothers and sisters?

The Seymour unicorn displaying the arms of Queen Jane Seymour, (part of the king's beasts at the entrance of Hampton Court Palace). (*Author's Collection*)

Who would he resemble? What would he be like when he grew up? What kind of King would he be? All these thoughts of the future would have filled her head and heart with happiness as she passed him to the care of his nurses while she rested and recovered … cruelly, she knew her son for only twelve days.

JANE SEYMOUR.
Third queen of Henry the 8th king of England

Coloured engraving of Jane Seymour, eighteenth/nineteenth century.

I enjoy a good ghost story as much as anyone but I don't have a firm opinion on their existence. I did not visit expecting to see or hear anything; I was simply happy to be there and pay my respects. As I knelt there though I had the strangest feeling. The best way to describe it is that it felt like Jane was just on the other side of a closed door, not a woman who had lived and died nearly 500 years ago and had been laid to rest nearby; for a moment she really felt that close. At the end of the day, visiting her grave is the closest we will ever come to standing beside her.

Jane Seymour, New York Public Library, c. 1738.

I stayed a few more minutes and, as I turned to leave, found myself feeling both happy and sad. I was happy that I had had the chance to visit and pay my respects but I was also sad and I'm still unsure why – perhaps it is as simple as sadness for potential that was lost too soon or perhaps I hadn't realised how attached to Jane I am. Perhaps both.

Chapter 10

Trivia

- Jane never received a coronation and neither would her successors – only Catherine of Aragon and Anne Boleyn were crowned. Chapuys recorded it was because Henry was waiting for Jane to prove she could produce a son but a surviving account from John Nedham, the clerk and surveyor general of the king's works, shows that work had begun at Westminster and the date of the event was to be 29 September 1536, the Feast of Michaelmas. It was postponed as the plague was circulating. It was later rescheduled for 31 October but this was also postponed because of the Pilgrimage of Grace.[1]

- The Seymours altered their family crest just before or just after Jane's marriage to the king. The original crest featured a peacock's head and neck with its wings in mid-flight but a peacock was a recognised symbol of pride and hardly what Jane wished to convey to the people around her. Instead, the peacock was altered to become a phoenix, which

Design for a cup for Jane Seymour by the workshop of Hans Holbein the Younger, c. 1536/7, possibly a wedding or Christmas gift.

symbolised resurrection, hope, sacrifice and rebirth. Jane's personal badge as queen was a phoenix rising from a castle surrounded by Tudor roses. The Tudor roses symbolised her marriage and hope for children with the king. Her personal motto as queen was 'Bound to Obey and Serve'.[2]

- During her marriage Jane received an exquisite gold cup from her husband. Designed by Hans Holbein, it displayed Henry and Jane's initials intertwined with love knots and her motto as queen; this full description comes the British Museum's website: 'with cover surmounted by two putti supporting a crowned shield, two mermaids beneath and the queen's motto, bands of intricate scrolling and in the centre a nude bust of a woman with masks in relief either side, below are the king's and queen's initials entwined, and gem-set Tudor roses, the stem decorated with pearl drops, dolphins and the queen's motto "BOUND TO OBEY [AND SERVE]".' Sadly, the cup was either sold or melted down for funds during the reign of Charles I but a replica was commissioned from Holbein's surviving designs by Sir Watkin Williams-Wynn, 6th Baronet of Wynnstay, in the 1800s.[3]
- The Seymours' name has been written as 'Semel',[4] 'St Maur',[5] 'Semer'[6] or possibly 'Seamowre'.[7] On coins Jane's initial was represented by the letter 'I' as there was no 'J' in Latin.[8] Her Christian name has been written as Jane, Joan,[9 & 10] June,[11] J(I)oanna,[12] and J(I)eanne as well.[13]
- In August 1537, a Dr Smythe found himself in trouble with the king's council for preaching a sermon that ended with him praying for the king and 'the lady jane late queen'. Jane was still very much alive in August 1537 and this unhappy event must have been the result of malicious gossip.[14]
- During Jane's time as queen the dissolution of the monasteries accelerated but in December 1537, Henry granted a charter for the

A replica of a coin minted during Jane's reign as queen. (*Author's Collection*)

The reverse of the same coin showing 'H' and 'I', Henry's and Jane's initials. (*Author's Collection*)

The Family of Henry VIII by an unknown artist, c. 1545. From left: 'Mother Jak', Lady Mary, Prince Edward, Henry VIII, Jane Seymour, Lady Elizabeth and Will Somers, Henry's fool. Jane had been dead for eight years when this portrait was painted; the Queen of England at the time was Catherine Parr. Jane continued to appear posthumously in portraits for the rest of Henry's life.

refoundation of a monastery at Bisham. The new monastery was to consist of one abbot and thirteen monks of the Benedictine order who were to pray for the good estate of the king and for the soul of the late queen consort, Jane; perhaps he did it in her honour but if he did, it would be short-lived as it was dissolved permanently on 19 June 1538.[15]

- Jane continued to appear in portraits well after her death; the most famous example, *The Family of Henry VIII*, was painted in 1545 when Catherine Parr was queen. In an inventory of Henry's belongings, it was discovered he had kept some of Jane's belongings including her dresses. Whilst clothing and jewellery were expensive and often passed on, it is only Jane's dresses and portraits that are recorded in his own possession at his death.[16]

- Jane has often been misidentified as England's first Protestant queen, probably because of her son's later fervent Protestantism; however, this is completely untrue. Jane remained a sincere Catholic until the end of her days and expressed concern about the fate of the monasteries; one of her goals as queen was to return Henry to Rome, one of her few failures. England's first Protestant queen was actually her successor but two, Catherine Parr.

- Puerperal fever killed a lot of women in Tudor England and this fact is cruelly represented in Henry's own family. His mother, Elizabeth of

York, and two of his wives, Jane Seymour and Catherine Parr, are believed to have died of it.

- Edward had mementos of the mother he never knew. He kept a comb, some documents, an enamelled glass depicting Christ's Passion, unicorn horns and, most extraordinarily of all, 'small tools of sorcery' – what they were we don't know.[17]

- In the *Letters and Papers, Foreign and Domestic Henry VIII* there is an interesting record of Henry having a vision of Jane after her death. An entry dated 10 August 1538

IOHANNA SEYMOVR REGINA HENRI ci VIII Regis Angliæ Vxor 3: Edwardi 6 Mater

Holbein pinxit.   W. Hollar fecit aqua forti   ex Collectione Arundeliana 1648.

Jane Seymour by Wenceslas Hollar, date unknown.

records the examinations of four men in connection with a rumour about pilgrimages. The rumour stated that an angel had appeared to Henry and told him to go on pilgrimage to St Michael's Mount and offer a noble there upon pain of death, and that 'queen Jane did appear to him and desired him to go on the same pilgrimage'.[18]

- It is rumoured that Jane has never really left Hampton Court Palace. On the anniversary of Edward's birth, a pale woman dressed in a white robe has been seen walking in the grounds of Clock Court. Carrying a candle, she climbs the stairs leading to the Silver Stick Gallery, which once led to Jane's rooms and the site of her greatest triumph, then vanishes.[19]

Notes

Chapter 1: The Seymour Family
1. David Loades, *The Seymours of Wolf Hall*, pp. 23–4
2. Ibid., p. 25
3. Ibid., p. 27
4. Ibid., p. 28
5. Ibid., p. 29
6. Ibid., p. 29
7. Ibid., p. 31
8. Ibid., p. 32
9. Ibid., p. 33

Chapter 2: Lady Jane Seymour
1. David Loades, *The Seymours of Wolf Hall*, p. 34
2. Elizabeth Norton, *Jane Seymour: Henry VIII's True Love*, pp. 8–10
3. David Loades, *The Seymours of Wolf Hall*, pp. 36–7
4. David Loades, *Jane Seymour: Henry VIII's Favourite Wife*, pp. 21–2
5. Elizabeth Norton, *Jane Seymour: Henry VIII's True Love*, p. 11
6. David Loades, *Jane Seymour: Henry VIII's Favourite Wife*, p. 23
7. www.historyofparliamentonline.org/volume/1509-1558/member/seymour-sir-henry-1503-78
8. David Loades, *The Seymours of Wolf Hall*, pp. 180–1
9. https://tudorsdynasty.com/the-other-seymours-dorothy-seymour-smith-leventhorpe/
10. *Letters and Papers, Foreign and Domestic, Henry VIII, Volume 10, January–June 1536*. Letter 901 – Chapuys to Antoine Perrenot, 18 May 1536
11. Elizabeth Norton, *Jane Seymour: Henry VIII's True Love*, pp. 11–12
12. Ibid., p. 80
13. David Loades, *Jane Seymour: Henry VIII's Favourite Wife*, p. 25
14. Elizabeth Norton, *Jane Seymour: Henry VIII's True Love*, pp. 12–13
15. Pamela M. Gross & the Duke of Somerset, *Jane the Quene, Third Consort of King Henry VIII, Studies in British History*, appendix XV
16. https://queenanneboleyn.com/2019/08/18/all-that-glitters-hans-holbeins-lady-of-the-cromwell-family-by-teri-fitzgerald/

Chapter 3: At Court
1. Elizabeth Norton, *Jane Seymour: Henry VIII's True Love,* pp. 17–18
2. Ibid.

3. *Letters and Papers, Foreign and Domestic, Henry VIII, Volume 2, 1515–1518*. Letter 1585 – the Venetian Ambassador to the Council of Ten, 24 February 1516
4. Elizabeth Norton, *Jane Seymour: Henry VIII's True Love*, p. 20

Chapter 4: The King's Great Matter
1. www.medievalists.net/2013/04/empress-matilda-lady-of-the-english/
2. www.tudorsociety.com/henry-fitzroy-1st-duke-of-richmond-and-somerset/
3. Undated letter from Margaret of Austria to Sir Thomas Boleyn, www.tudortimes.co.uk
4. The diplomat Lancelot de Carles – 'a native-born Frenchwoman', http://sarahgristwood.com
5. www.theanneboleynfiles.com/1st-march-1522-anne-boleyn-plays-perseverance/
6. George Cavendish, *The Life of Cardinal Wolsey*
7. Elizabeth Norton, *Jane Seymour: Henry VIII's True Love*, p. 22
8. Ibid., p. 26
9. David Starkey, *Six Wives: The Queens of Henry VIII*, p. 241
10. George Cavendish, *Life of Cardinal Wolsey*. https://thetudortravelguide.com/2019/06/08/blackfriars/

Chapter 5: Cinderella
1. George Cavendish, *The Life of Cardinal Wolsey*
2. *Letters and Papers, Foreign and Domestic, Henry VIII, Volume 5, 1531–1532*. Letter 361 – Chapuys to Charles V, 31 July 1531
3. Ibid., Letter 416 – Chapuys to Charles V, 10 September 1531
4. *Letters and Papers, Foreign and Domestic, Henry VIII, Volume 6, 1533*. Letter 324 – Chapuys to Charles V, 10 April 1533
5. *Letters and Papers, Foreign and Domestic, Henry VIII, Volume 7, 1534*. Document 9 – New Year's Gifts, 1 January 1534
6. Edward Hall, *Hall's Chronicle*
7. *Miscellaneous writings and letters of Thomas Cranmer*, edited by Rev. John Edmund Cox
8. Edward Hall, *Hall's Chronicle*
9. Eric Ives, *The Life and Death of Anne Boleyn: The Most Happy*, p. 158
10. Elizabeth Norton, *Jane Seymour: Henry VIII's True Love*, pp. 41–2
11. David Loades, *Jane Seymour: Henry VIII's Favourite Wife*, p. 28
12. *Inquisitions Post Mortem c. 142/46/25*, Sir William Fillol, 19 Hen. VIII. P. R. O.
13. Henry Clifford, E. E Estcourt & Joseph Stevenson, *The Life of Jane Dormer, Duchess of Feria*
14. Ibid.
15. Chris Skidmore, *Edward VI: The Lost King of England*

Chapter 6: Catching the King's Eye
1. *Letters and Papers, Foreign and Domestic, Henry VIII, Volume 6, 1533.* Letter 1069 – Chapuys to Charles V, 3 September 1533
2. *Letters and Papers, Foreign and Domestic, Henry VIII, Volume 7, 1534.* Letter 1193 – Chapuys to Charles V, 27 September 1534
3. *Letters and Papers, Foreign and Domestic, Henry VIII, Volume 8, January–July 1535.* Document 989, 5 July 1535
4. https://thetudortravelguide.com/2018/10/20/the-resurrection-of-wolf-hall/
5. www.theanneboleynfiles.com/henry-viii-anne-boleyns-1535-royal-progress/
6. Amy Licence, *The Six Wives and Many Mistresses of Henry VIII*, p. 263
7. Elizabeth Norton, *Jane Seymour Henry VIII's True Love*, pp. 52–53
8. Amy Licence, *The Six Wives and Many Mistresses of Henry VIII*, p. 264
9. Alison Weir, *The Six Wives of Henry VIII*, pp. 295–296
10. *Letters and Papers, Foreign and Domestic, Henry VIII Volume 10, January–June 1536.* Letter 28 – Sir Edmund Bedingfield to Thomas Cromwell, 5 January 1536
11. Giles Tremlett, *Catherine of Aragon: The Spanish Queen of Henry VIII*, p. 364
12. *Letters and Papers, Foreign and Domestic, Henry VIII, Volume 10, January–June 1536.* Letter 141 – Chapuys to Charles V, 21 January 1536
13. Amy Licence, *The Six Wives and Many Mistresses of Henry VIII*, p. 265
14. www.theanneboleynfiles.com/anne-boleyn-and-bloody-mary/
15. https://thefreelancehistorywriter.com/2018/04/06/the-funeral-of-catherine-of-aragon/
16. *Letters and Papers, Foreign and Domestic, Henry VIII, Volume 10, January–June 1536.* Letter 282 – Chapuys to Charles V, 10 February 1536
17. Henry Clifford, E. E Estcourt & Joseph Stevenson, *The Life of Jane Dormer, Duchess of Feria*
18. Alison Weir, *The Six Wives of Henry VIII*, pp. 303–4
19. J. E. Neale, *Queen Elizabeth I*
20. Alison Weir, *The Six Wives of Henry VIII*, p. 304
21. *Letters and Papers, Foreign and Domestic, Henry VIII, Volume 10, January–June 1536.* Letter 199 – Chapuys to Charles V, 29 January 1536
22. Elizabeth Norton, *Jane Seymour Henry VIII's True love*, pp. 57–8
23. Ibid.
24. *Letters and Papers, Foreign and Domestic, Henry VIII, Volume 10, January–June 1536.* Letter 495– Chapuys to Charles V, 18 March 1536
25. Ibid., Letter 601 – Chapuys to Charles V, 1 April 1536
26. James Orchard Halliwell Phillips, *Letters of the Kings of England, Volume 1*, p. 353.
27. *Letters and Papers, Foreign and Domestic, Henry VIII, Volume 10, January–June 1536.* Document 715 – The Garter
28. Ibid., Letter 752 – Chapuys to Charles V, 29 April 1536

29. Ibid., Letter 601 – Chapuys to Charles V, 1 April 1536
30. Ibid., Letter 699 – Chapuys to Charles V, 21 April 1536
31. Ibid., Letter 720 – Chapuys to Granvelle, 24 April 1536
32. Ibid., Letter 793 – Sir William Kingston to Thomas Cromwell, 3 May 1536
33. www.hevercastle.co.uk/news/19th-may-anniversary-of-anne-boleyns-execution/#:~:text=Anne%20Boleyn's%20Final%20Words&text=I%20am%20come%20hither%20to,a%20gentle%2C%20and%20sovereign%20lord.
34. *The Chronicle of King Henry VIII. of England,* sometimes known as the *Spanish Chronicle* is a chronicle written during the reigns of Henry VIII and Edward VI by an unknown author.

Chapter 7: The Third Quene

1. *Letters and Papers, Foreign and Domestic, Henry VIII, Volume 10, January–June 1536.* Letter 908 – Chapuys to Charles V, 19 May 1536
2. Ibid.
3. Ibid.
4. *Letters and Papers, Foreign and Domestic, Henry VIII, Volume 10, January–June 1536.* Letter 926 – Chapuys to Granvelle- 20tyh May 1536
5. *Letters and Papers, Foreign and Domestic, Henry VIII, Volume 11, July–December 1536.* Letter 29 – Thomas Cromwell to Bishop Gardiner, 5 July 1536
6. *Chronicle of King Henry VIII of England/ Spanish Chronicle*
7. Elizabeth Norton, *Jane Seymour: Henry VIII's True Wife,* p. 80
8. *Letters and Papers, Foreign and Domestic, Henry VIII Volume 10 January–June 1536.* Letter 1047 – Sir John Russell to Lord Lisle, 3 June 1536
9. Ibid., Letter 1069 – Chapuys to Charles V, 6 June 1536
10. *A Chronicle of England During the Reigns of the Tudors, From A.D. 1485 to 1559,* better known as *Wriothesley's Chronicle,* was written during the reigns of Henry VIII, Edward VI, Mary I and Elizabeth I, by Charles Wriothesley.
11. *Letters and Papers, Foreign and Domestic Henry VIII Volume 10 January–June 1536.* Letter 901 – Chapuys to Antoine Perrenot 18 May 1536
12. Elizabeth Norton, *Jane Seymour: Henry's True Love,* p. 82
13. Ibid., p. 94
14. *Letter and Papers, Foreign and Domestic Henry VIII Volume 10 January–June 1536.* Letter 1136 – Princess Mary to Henry VIII, 15 June 1536
15. Ibid., Letter 1203 – Princess Mary to Henry VIII, 26 June 1536
16. Elizabeth Norton, *Jane Seymour: Henry's True Love,* pp 96–7
17. Ibid., p. 99
18. Lauren Mackay, *Inside the Tudor Court: Henry VIII and His Six Wives Through the Writings of the Spanish Ambassador Eustace Chapuys*
19. Sylvia Barbara Soberton has found evidence that Jane actually paid more attention to Elizabeth than first thought. See *Rival Sisters: Mary and Elizabeth Tudor*

20. www.luminarium.org/encyclopedia/tenarticles.htm
21. Elizabeth Norton, *Jane Seymour: Henry's True Love*, p. 107
22. Ibid., p. 109
23. Ibid., p. 106
24. Ibid., p. 111
25. Pamela M. Gross & the Duke of Somerset, *Jane the Quene, Third Consort of King Henry VIII*, Studies in British History, appendix XVIII
26. *Letters and Papers, Foreign and Domestic, Henry VIII, Volume 11, July–December 1536*. R. O. St. Pap. i. 463, 19 October 1536
27. Elizabeth Norton, *Jane Seymour: Henry's True Love*, p. 118
28. *Letters and Papers, Foreign and Domestic, Henry VIII, Volume 11, July–December 1536*. Letter 860 – to the Cardinal du Bellay, 24 October 1536
29. https://archive.org/details/wiltshiretopogra00aubr/page/374/mode/2up?view=theater
30. *Letters and Papers, Foreign and Domestic, Henry VIII, Volume 12 Part 1, January–May 1537*. Letters 322, 362, 369, 380, 401, 402, 416, 466, 473, 532, 533, 534
31. Elizabeth Norton, *Jane Seymour: Henry's True Love*, p. 122
32. *Letters and Papers, Foreign and Domestic, Henry VIII, Volume 12 Part 1, January–May 1537*. Letter 1187 – John Husee to Lord Lisle, 12 May 1537; letter 1188 – John Husee to Lady Lisle, 12 May 1537; letter 1266 – John Husee to Lord Lisle, 23 May 1537; letter 1267 – John Husee to Lady Lisle, 23 May 1537; and document 1325 – A Sermon at Oxford.
33. *Letters and Papers, Foreign and Domestic, Henry VIII, Volume 12 Part 2, June–December 1537*. Letter 22 – Norfolk to Cromwell, 3 June 1537

Chapter 8: Triumph and Disaster

1. *Letters and Papers, Foreign and Domestic, Henry VIII, Volume 12 Part 1, January–May 1537*. Letter 709 – Henry VIII to the Duke of Norfolk, 24 March 1537
2. Ibid., Letter 1069 – John Husee to Lady Lisle, 30 April 1537
3. Elizabeth Norton, *Jane Seymour: Henry VIII's True Love*, pp 137–8
4. *Letters and Papers, Foreign and Domestic, Henry VIII, Volume 12 Part 1, January–May 1537*. Document 1325 – A Sermon at Oxford
5. Ibid., Letter 1266 – John Husee to Lord Lisle, 23 May 1537
6. Ibid., Letter 696 – Instructions issued by Charles V to Don Diego de Mendoça and the Señor de Arbes sent to England, 22 March 1537
7. Elizabeth Norton, *Jane Seymour: Henry VIII's True Love*, p. 133
8. Ibid.
9. https://tudortimes.co.uk/guest-articles/tudor-beauty-ideals/jane-seymour
10. *Letters and Papers, Foreign and Domestic, Henry VIII, Volume 12 Part 2, June–December 1537*. Letter 242 – Sir J. Russell to Cromwell, 11 July 1537
11. Ibid., Letter 298 – John Husee to Lady Lisle, 21 July 1537
12. Elizabeth Norton, *Jane Seymour: Henry VIII's True Love*, p. 140

13. Charles Wriothesley, *Wriothesley's Chronicle*
14. Henry Ellis, *The Love letters of Henry VIII and Anne Boleyn & other correspondence & documents concerning the King and his wives*, p. 74
15. *Letters and Papers, Foreign and Domestic, Henry VIII, Volume 12 Part 2, June–December 1537*. Document 911 – 'The christening of Prince Edward, the most dearest son of King Henry the VIIIth of yt name', 15 October 1537
16. Agnes Strickland, *Lives of the Queens of England: From the Norman Conquest, Volumes 4–5*
17. www.flickr.com/photos/20631910@N03/3735007711/in/faves-192773142@N04/
18. *Letters and Papers, Foreign and Domestic, Henry VIII, Volume 12 Part 2, June–December 1537*. Letter 977 – Sir J. Russell to Cromwell, 24 October 1537
19. https://tudortimes.co.uk/people/jane-seymour
20. *Letters and Papers, Foreign and Domestic, Henry VIII, Volume 12 Part 2, June–December* 1537. Letter 971 – Duke of Norfolk to Cromwell, 24 October 1537
21. Ibid., Letter 970 – Earl of Rutland, Bishop of Carlisle and others to Cromwell, 24 October 1537
22. Ibid., Letter 1004 – Thomas Cromwell to Lord William Howard and Gardiner, October 1537
23. https://tudortimes.co.uk/guest-articles/why-did-jane-seymour-die-in-childbed
24. www.theanneboleynfiles.com/did-jane-seymour-have-a-c-section/
25. Ibid.
26. www.sacred-texts.com/neu/eng/child/ch170.htm
27. https://en.wikipedia.org/wiki/The_Death_of_Queen_Jane
28. Alison Weir, *The Six Wives of Henry VIII*, p. 371
29. *Letters and Papers, Foreign and Domestic, Henry VIII, Volume 12 Part 2, June–December 1537*. Letter 1060 – A remembrance of the interment of Queen Jane, mother of Edward VI., who died at Hampton Court, 24 Oct., on Wednesday about 12 p. m., in child-bed, 29 Henry VIII, 12 November 1537
30. Pamela M. Gross & the Duke of Somerset, *Jane the Quene, Third Consort of King Henry VIII*, Studies in British History, p. 74
31. Charles Wriothesley, *Wriothesley's Chronicle*
32. Amy Licence, *The Six Wives and Many Mistresses of Henry VIII*, p. 290
33. See note 29.
34. https://michelemorrical.com/the-funeral-of-queen-elizabeth-of-york/
35. https://thefreelancehistorywriter.com/2014/04/03/the-funeral-of-queen-elizabeth-of-york-the-first-tudor-queen-of-england/
36. See note 29.

Chapter 9: After Jane

1. *Letters and Papers, Foreign and Domestic, Henry VIII, Volume 12 Part 2, June–December 1537*. Letter 972 – Henry VIII to Francis I, 24 October 1537

2. Ibid. Letter 1067 – Thomas Knyght to Cromwell, 12 November 1537
3. Ibid. Letter 1030 – Norfolk to Cromwell, 4 November 1537
4. Ibid. Document 973 – 'A book of the Quenes juelles'.
5. Ibid. Document 974, 24 October 1537
6. Ibid. Letter 1004 – Thomas Cromwell to Lord William Howard and Gardiner, October 1537
7. Ibid. Letter 1188 – John Hutton to Charles Wriothesley, 9 December 1537
8. Derek Wilson, *Hans Holbein: Portrait of an Unknown Man*
9. Antonia Fraser, *Mary Queen of Scots*, p. 7
10. Kelly Hart, *The Mistresses of Henry VIII*, p. 172
11. https://warmdayswillnevercease.wordpress.com/2021/03/08/catherine-parr-queen-and-writer/
12. Alison Weir, *The Six Wives of Henry VIII*, p. 530
13. *Letters and Papers, Foreign and Domestic, Henry VIII, Volume 21 Part 2, September 1546–January 1547.* Document 634 – Henry VIII.'s Will, 30 December 1546
14. Jennifer Loach, *Edward VI* (The Yale English Monarch Series), quoting *Edward VI's Chronicle*
15. Chris Skidmore, *Edward VI: The Lost King of England*
16. www.westminster-abbey.org/abbey-commemorations/royals/edward-vi
17. David Loades, *The Seymours of Wolf Hall*, pp. 167–8
18. Alison Weir, *The Six Wives of Henry VIII*, p. 374
19. Alison Weir, *Henry VIII: King and Court*, p. 219
20. Ibid., p. 297
21. https://royalcentral.co.uk/features/looking-for-the-grave-of-queen-jane-seymour-127948/
22. www.tudorsociety.com/a-tomb-fit-for-a-king-benedettos-candelabra-for-henry-viii/
23. www.stgeorges-windsor.org/image_of_the_month/henry-viiis-tomb/
24. www.vam.ac.uk/content/articles/w/wolsey-angels-appeal/
25. https://londonist.com/london/secrets-of-syon-house-and-park
26. www.theanneboleynfiles.com/31st-march-1532-friar-petos-easter-sermon/
27. Henry Halford, *An account of the opening of the tomb of Charles I*
28. www.stgeorges-windsor.org/wp-content/uploads/2017/08/BackgroundNotesHenryVIII.pdf
29. Ibid., p. 21

Chapter 10: Trivia

1. https://tudorsdynasty.com/the-plague-of-1536-7-and-jane-seymours-delayed-coronation/
2. www.theanneboleynfiles.com/jane-seymour-redefining-the-myth/
3. www.britishmuseum.org/collection/object/P_1848-1125-9
4. *Letters and Papers, Foreign and Domestic, Henry VIII, Volume 10, January–June 1536.* Letter 901 – Chapuys to Antoine Perrenot, 18 May 1536

5. Elizabeth Norton, *Jane Seymour: Henry VIII's True Love*, p. 7

6. *Letters and Papers, Foreign and Domestic, Henry VIII, Volume 12 Part 2, June–December 1537*. Document 911 – 'The christening of Prince Edward, the most dearest son of King Henry the VIIIth of yt name', 15 October 1537

7. *Letters and Papers, Foreign and Domestic, Henry VIII, Volume 12 Part 2, June–December 1537*. Document 973 – 'A book of the Quenes juelles'

8. https://how-ocr-works.com/languages/latin-alphabet.html

9. *Letters and Papers, Foreign and Domestic, Henry VIII, Volume 12 Part 1, January–May 1537*. Document 311 – GRANTS IN JANUARY 1537.

10. Ibid., Letter 795 – GRANTS IN MARCH 1537 – GRANT 45

11. *Letters and Papers, Foreign and Domestic, Henry VIII, Volume 12 Part 2, June–December 1537*. Document 617 – GRANTS IN AUGUST 1537

12. See image p. 169

13. See image p. 43

14. *Letters and Papers, Foreign and Domestic, Henry VIII, Volume 12 Part 2, June–December 1537*. Letter 534 – Walter Walsshe, Ric. Tracy, and Wm. Robynson to Cromwell, 18 August 1537

15. *Letters and Papers, Foreign and Domestic, Henry VIII, Volume 12 Part 2, June–December 1537*. Document 1311 – GRANTS IN DECEMBER 1537 – GRANT 22

16. Linda Collins, Siobhan Clarke, *King and Collector: Henry VIII and the Art of Kingship*

17. David Loades, *Jane Seymour: Henry's VIII's Favourite Wife*, pp. 131–2, p. 176

18. *Letters and Papers, Foreign and Domestic, Henry VIII, Volume 13 Part 2, August–December 1538*. Document 62 – Rumours of Pilgrimages, 10 August 1538

19. www.hrp. org.uk/hampton-court-palace/history-and-stories/historic-hauntings-at-hampton-court-palace/#gs.79pph3

Bibliography

Books

Collins, Linda & Clarke, Siobhan, *King and Collector: Henry VIII and the Art of Kingship*, The History Press, Cheltenham, 2021.

Gross, Pamela M. & the Duke of Somerset, *Jane the Quene, Third Consort of King Henry VIII Studies in British History*, Edwin Mellen Press Ltd, Lampeter, 1999.

Licence, Amy, *The Six Wives & Many Mistresses of Henry VIII: The Women's Stories*, Amberley Publishing, Gloucestershire, 2014.

Loades, David, *Jane Seymour: Henry VIII's Favourite Wife*, Amberley Publishing, Gloucestershire, 2013.

Loades, David, *The Seymours of Wolf Hall*, Amberley Publishing, Gloucestershire, 2017.

Mackay, Lauren, *Inside the Tudor Court: Henry VIII and His Six Wives Through the writings of the Spanish Ambassador Eustace Chapuys*, Amberley Publishing, Gloucestershire, 2014.

Norton, Elizabeth, *Jane Seymour: Henry VIII's True Love*, Amberley Publishing, Gloucestershire, 2009.

Skidmore, Chris, *Edward VI: The Lost King of England*, W&N Publishing, London, 2008

Soberton, Sylvia Barbara, *Medical Downfall of the Tudors: Sex, Reproduction and Succession*, independently published, 2020.

Soberton, Sylvia Barbara, *Rival Sisters: Mary and Elizabeth Tudor*, independently published, 2019.

Weir, Alison, *The Six Wives of Henry VIII*, Vintage Publishing, London, 2007.

Online Sources

British History Online. Letters and Papers, Foreign and Domestic Henry VIII: www.british-history.ac.uk/search/series/letters-papers-hen8

Larson, Rebecca Tudors Dynasty: https://tudorsdynasty.com/

www.luminarium.org/

Acknowledgements

My most sincere thanks to Sarah-Beth Watkins and Claire Hopkins for giving me the opportunity to write this book; also, to Tracy Borman and Alison Weir for taking time out of their busy schedules to respond to my emails.

Index